Picturebooks and Literary Understanding,
in Honour of Lawrence Sipe

Margaret Mackey
Editor

Picturebooks and Literary Understanding, in Honour of Lawrence Sipe

Previously published in the journal *Children's Literature in Education,* Volume 43, Issue 1, 2012

 Springer

Editor
Margaret Mackey
Dept. of Secondary Education
University of Alberta
Edmonton
Canada
margaret.mackey@ualberta.ca

ISBN: 978-94-007-4323-6

Springer Dordrecht Heidelberg New York London

Library of Congress Control Number: 2012934257

© Springer Science+Business Media Dodrecht 2012
This work is subject to copyright. All rights are reserved by the Publisher, whether the whole or part of the material is concerned, specifically the rights of translation, reprinting, reuse of illustrations, recitation, broadcasting, reproduction on microfilms or in any other physical way, and transmission or information storage and retrieval, electronic adaptation, computer software, or by similar or dissimilar methodology now known or hereafter developed. Exempted from this legal reservation are brief excerpts in connection with reviews or scholarly analysis or material supplied specifically for the purpose of being entered and executed on a computer system, for exclusive use by the purchaser of the work. Duplication of this publication or parts thereof is permitted only under the provisions of the Copyright Law of the Publisher's location, in its current version, and permission for use must always be obtained from Springer. Permissions for use may be obtained through RightsLink at the Copyright Clearance Center. Violations are liable to prosecution under the respective Copyright Law.
The use of general descriptive names, registered names, trademarks, service marks, etc. in this publication does not imply, even in the absence of a specific statement, that such names are exempt from the relevant protective laws and regulations and therefore free for general use.
While the advice and information in this book are believed to be true and accurate at the date of publication, neither the authors nor the editors nor the publisher can accept any legal responsibility for any errors or omissions that may be made. The publisher makes no warranty, express or implied, with respect to the material contained herein.

Printed on acid-free paper

Springer is part of Springer Science+Business Media (www.springer.com)

Contents

Editor's Note	*Margaret Mackey*	1
Revisiting the Relationships Between Text and Pictures	*Lawrence R. Sipe*	4
Children's Literature *and* Education: A Memoir of Dr. Lawrence Sipe	*Rachel Skrlac Lo*	22
Navigating Worlds of "Trouble and Woe and Worse" in Children's Literature: An Exploration into the Double Text of Tony Kushner and Maurice Sendak's *Brundibar*	*Kristin M. Larsen*	27
A Blissful Education	*David Low*	48
Exploring Grade 7 Students' Responses to Shaun Tan's *The Red Tree*	*Sylvia Pantaleo*	51
Retelling and Remembering: In Honor of Dr. Lawrence Sipe	*Danielle Gioia*	72
Towards a Culturally Situated Reader Response Theory	*Wanda Brooks and Susan Browne*	74
A Tribute to Dr. Sipe's Memory: Recounting His Final Lessons Teaching Young Adult Fiction, Spring 2011	*Emily Sokol*	86
Reading Picturebooks *as Literature*: Four-to-Six-Year-Old Children and the Development of Literary Competence	*Coosje van der Pol*	93
Author Studies: An Effective Strategy for Engaging Pre-Service Teachers in the Study of Children's Literature	*Amy Kennedy*	107

Children's Literature in Education (2012) 43:1–3
DOI 10.1007/s10583-011-9159-7

EDITORIAL OF THE COMMEMORATIVE ISSUE FOR DR. LAWRENCE SIPE

Editor's Note

Margaret Mackey

Published online: 15 February 2012
© Springer Science+Business Media, LLC 2012

It is my sad honour to present a special issue of *Children's Literature in Education* devoted to celebrating and commemorating the life and work of Larry Sipe— Dr. Lawrence R. Sipe—who was the North American Editor-in-Chief of this journal

---

Margaret Mackey is a Professor in the School of Library and Information Studies at the University of Alberta. She served as North American Editor-in-Chief of *Children's Literature in Education* between 1996 and 2007.

This is the editorial note for the articles listed below pertaining to the Special issue titled "Commemorative Issue for Dr. Lawrence Sipe" 10.1007/s10583-011-9149-9, 10.1007/s10583-011-9150-3, 10.1007/s10583-011-9151-2, 10.1007/s10583-011-9152-1, 10.1007/s10583-011-9153-0, 10.1007/s10583-011-9154-z, 10.1007/s10583-011-9155-y, 10.1007/s10583-011-9156-x, 10.1007/s10583-011-9157-9, 10.1007/s10583-011-9158-8.

M. Mackey (✉)
School of Library and Information Studies, University of Alberta, 3-20 Rutherford South, Edmonton, AB T6G 2J4, Canada
e-mail: mmackey@ualberta.ca; margaret.mackey@ualberta.ca

between 2006 and his sudden and untimely death in March 2011. Special issues are exceptionally rare in the publishing history of *CLE*—but Larry brought exceptional qualities to this journal, both as a highly esteemed contributor and as a valued editor.

When we announced the commemorative issue, we were braced for many submissions, all needing to be processed within a very tight timeline. I wrote to every *CLE* reviewer, asking who could volunteer to turn articles around in very short order at a busy time of the year. I was deluged with replies from people eager to help and also to acknowledge Larry's importance in their own lives and their own scholarship. Similar accolades poured in with the expected rush of submissions. Combined with the tributes on Facebook and on the website set up by Larry's home institution of the Graduate School of Education at the University of Pennsylvania, these eloquent acknowledgments could fill a special issue all by themselves. It has been a privilege to read them, knowing how touched Larry would have been to register the impact and quality of his influence.

In this issue of the journal, I have done my best to reflect the broad range of Larry's contribution to the field that can precisely be described as "children's literature in education." In its pages you will find an analysis and history of a single picturebook, reports of work with young readers of picturebooks, and theoretical exploration of how we may better understand issues of reading and of culture through attending carefully to the responses of such readers. Interspersed with these full-length articles are heartfelt reflections by Larry's students, present and past. The issue concludes with an article by a former student who is applying some of Larry's teaching craft in her own college classrooms; it seemed appropriate to finish with a sense that the work goes on.

Taking pride of place at the beginning of the issue is an unfinished piece by Larry himself—a reminder of what the field has lost and perhaps an impetus for another scholar to take up the challenge of providing an overview of our current understanding of the interpretation of picturebooks. Lee Galda, who was working on a book with Larry at the time of his death, has provided this manuscript and done the minimal editing she decided was appropriate. It was Lee who initially suggested this special issue and she has supported and improved it in ways too numerous to mention.

In addition to thanking Lee wholeheartedly, I would also like to express my gratitude to all the other editors of *CLE*, new and old, North American and European. This project has truly been a team effort. Many members of the North American editorial board also offered support far beyond the bounds of reasonable expectation. The technical personnel at Springer have been very helpful in finding ways to tweak the normal publication routines so that all these pieces can be presented together, both online and in paper.

Not every article could be accepted or reworked within the limits of the very tight schedule or the strict ration of pages. Look for some of these articles to appear in subsequent issues of *CLE*. I have never found it harder to write letters of rejection. As a rule, sending suggestions for editorial improvement is a positive job, but in this case, requesting time-consuming revisions meant that some authors would simply not be able to meet the deadline for the special issue. Those letters too were very difficult to write. The personal investment of every submitting author was very clear and very moving.

If it is true that we may know a man by his friends, then working on this commemorative issue has reminded me (not that I needed it) that Larry Sipe was a special man indeed. The quality of scholarship informed by his work is matched by the personal testimonials. I hope this issue provides some sense of the scale of his legacy.

COMMEMORATIVE ISSUE FOR DR. LAWRENCE SIPE

Revisiting the Relationships Between Text and Pictures

Lawrence R. Sipe

Published online: 15 February 2012
© Springer Science+Business Media, LLC 2012

This article was originally part of the introduction to and a chapter for a book proposed by Larry, tentatively titled Picturebooks: Visual and Verbal Art. Neither the proposal nor the chapter was finished at the time of his death. Rather than speak for him, we have decided to use only his own words, with minor editing, leaving the gaps that existed in this draft. In places where he made notes about other scholars he planned to consider, we indicate that using italics. We completed the references as best we could; where he mentioned only a name and an idea, we have included that, as is. It is our hope that this piece will be important to other scholars as they continue to explore text-picture relationships in picturebooks. The original draft was written in the summer of 2010, while Larry was at the University of Minnesota, Minneapolis, working with materials at the Kerlan Collection. This version was lightly edited by Lee Galda.

Picturebooks are highly sophisticated aesthetic objects, worthy of study and research by readers and viewers of all ages. As aesthetic wholes, picturebooks combine words and visual images (and occasionally other modalities) in complicated ways to produce this unity. Although there are several types of picturebooks, this article considers only picture storybooks—where there is a discernible narrative or several narratives—because the dynamics of picture storybooks are unique.

Scholarship and general interest in picturebooks continues to grow. The establishment of the Eric Carle Museum of Picture Book Art, which opened its doors in November, 2002, and such institutions as Seven Stories in the UK, opened in 2005, demonstrate a continuing burgeoning interest in this unique format—the only truly unique contribution of children's literature to the world of literary endeavor in general. Growth in scholarship and interest is also apparent in the

L. R. Sipe (✉)
University of Minnesota, Minneapolis, MN, USA

number of articles and books published on the subject in the past decade, and the concomitant development of an impressive body of research. A significant number of journals are devoted to children's literature, which often include articles specifically on picturebooks. Since 2000, much has happened to the world of picturebooks and picturebook scholarship, in addition to the thousands of new picturebooks that have been published during that period.

For some time, writers have considered that the complex ways in which visual images and verbal texts relate to each other constitute the *sine qua non* of the picturebook. Over the past 30 years, much has been written by scholars about these relationships; and author/illustrators such as Maurice Sendak and Joseph Schwarcz have been making intriguing and useful statements about words and pictures for even longer. Lewis (2001) comments that the picturebook as a whole seems to be "shared between two different forms of communication—words and pictures" (p. xii). Lewis's comment suggests that there are, indeed two different sets of languages in a picturebook: the language (in the usual sense) of the sequence of words and the language of the sequence of pictures. From a semiotic point of view, we can conceptualize these two languages as systems of "signs." For semioticians, everything and anything can function as sign; in picturebooks, the two most obvious sign systems are the words and the pictures, though within each of these broad sign systems, there are clearly sub-sign systems. For example, within the sign system of visual images, there is the sign system of colors, where different colors may be associated with different emotions or feelings. In any case, it is the way these sign systems interrelate, connect, and influence each other that is the object of scrutiny in this article.

Here, I revisit the ongoing scholarly conversation about words and pictures and extend it. I discuss the four main ways in which scholars, and others concerned with picturebooks (for example, authors, illustrators, designers, and editors) consider text–picture relationships. The first of these four perspectives is to think analogically: there are many *metaphors* (either extended or quite simple) that provide ways of viewing the relationships between words and pictures. Second, there are *theoretical constructs* that attempt to illuminate the "how" and "why" of word/picture associations. Third, there are a number of *typologies* or *taxonomies* that describe the diverse ways in which words and pictures interrelate in picturebooks. Lastly, some scholars and theorists, including myself, have taken *phenomenological approaches* to the question of word–picture connections, asking what goes on inside the minds of readers/viewers as they make sense of picturebooks. The basic premise of all these perspectives is that a picturebook can only be fully understood when readers/viewers understand the intricate and dynamic relationships between the sign system of the visual images and the sign system of the words.

Metaphors and Analogies

Perhaps the easiest and most natural way to talk about word–picture relationships is to use metaphors. We can hardly avoid metaphors when writing about word–picture relationships (or anything else, for that matter). Simply to say, for example, that pictures and words "work" together in various ways is already to be drawn into metaphorical thinking: if there is work involved, it is clearly not between words and pictures, but in the reader/viewer's mind, and it is the mental processes involved that constitute the work. Nevertheless, there has been no lack of inventiveness employed by writers who perceive the elegance and power of metaphorical thinking in this regard. Writers draw on the arts in many ways; they also utilize metaphors from science and technology in thinking about these relationships.

Metaphors from the Arts

Writers frequently employ metaphors from the various arts to convey the relationship of words and pictures in picturebooks. Terms and ideas drawn from music are quite frequently used. Maurice Sendak often writes of musical terms in his eloquent explanations of the dynamics of picturebooks. As he argues that Randolph Caldecott produced the first true picturebooks, he comments, "For in these two works [*Hey Diddle Diddle* and *Baby Bunting*] you find a rhythmic syncopation between words and images—a syncopation which is both delightful and highly musical" (Sendak in Cott, 1984, p. ix). Sendak goes on to state, "He [Caldecott] *reads* into things, and this is of course, what the illustrator's job is really all about—to interpret the text much as a musical conductor interprets a score… (I continually talk about the musical and contrapunctal quality of Caldecott's work because I literally hear music as I turn the pages!)" (p. x). In these passages, Sendak is using the term "rhythmic syncopation" which is "musical" and "contrapunctal." Others have followed Sendak's lead: Janet and Allan Ahlberg have referred to the "antiphonal" and "fugue"-like effects (cited in Moss, 1990) of the illustrations and words. "Counterpoint" (Pullman, 1989) also occurs with some frequency (of course related to the term "contrapunctal") (Ward and Fox, 1984), referring specifically to the words and pictures as two lines in a musical composition: "The technique of combining two or more melodic lines in such a way that they establish a harmonic relationship while retaining their linear individuality" (*The American Heritage Dictionary*). This definition introduces another term—"harmony"—into the musical metaphor, and this term is taken up by several other writers. For example, Cech (1983/1984) refers to the "duet" between words and pictures. This image implies that, just as in a musical duet, where at times one instrument dominates another in playing the melody while the other provides counterpoint, so too both instruments can play together with equal dominance. Thus, the image gestures towards various relationships that words and pictures can have with each other. In music, the various lines may appear momentarily in tension or conflict with each other, so "disharmony" or "dissonance" (Massey, 1980) is possible as well: words and pictures may appear to not interact positively together, or even to flatly contradict each other, just as various melodic musical lines may occasionally produce unusual or jarring juxtapositions.

Another of the arts that writers draw upon in discussing the relation of words and pictures is drama. Wyile (2006) provides an extended metaphor using the idea of a picturebook as a play:

The words in a picturebook are like the script of a play. In both cases the facts and clues of characters' feelings are not usually explained because the pictures or the actors can express them much better...The words in a picturebook come alive in relation to the pictures, as they do in relation to the action in a play. The effectiveness of words is related to their placement on the page in conjunction with the placement of the pictures, which is a form of artistic direction like the elements of direction and blocking in a play. The narrative tension is further created and/or enhanced by the pace of the production that is set by the timing of action, lighting, and sound effects in a play and by the combination of page layout and page turn in a picture book—typically the words pull us forward because we can read them faster and the pictures hold us back as our eyes scan for details (see Nodelman, 'How Picture Books Work') (p. 177).

According to Curley (2003), illustrator Nancy Ekholm Burkert "claims kinship between her work and a stage director's. 'I enjoy visualizing a literary work; illustration is like staging a play...designing the sets, the costumes, the lighting, "casting" the characters'" (p. 8). (See Spaulding, 1995 for a discussion of the likenesses of illustrations in a picturebook to a stage set, the costumed characters, and their non-verbal actions, while the words are the script, as in Wyile's comment, above.)

In another performance-related metaphor, author/illustrator Mini Grey writes that words and pictures constitute a "fantastic double act," as in vaudeville, which Sendak echoes when he refers to the complicated "funny kind of juggling act" of words and pictures (Sendak in Lanes, 1980, p. 110).

Some scholars compare words and pictures to the experience of a film, another form of "sequential art" (Eisner, 1979). Curley (2007) comments, "Each picture is married to the narrative, just as the film is interwoven with a soundtrack" (p. 11). In this passage Curley compares the continuous visual images of a film to the sequence of pictures in a picturebooks, and the soundtrack of the film to the words. This comparison makes the point that it is the sequence of words and visual images, in addition to the individual illustration or the accompanying set of words on a single opening, that comprise the word–picture relationship. The Caldecott-winning illustrator David Wiesner says that he must keep the whole sequence of words and pictures in mind when he works on any one double page spread (Wiesner, 2010, p. 254). Nodelman (1988), in *Words about Pictures*, also makes comparisons between films and picturebooks, using such cinematic terminology as the "establishing shot" (p. x).

Finally, a few writers use metaphors of textiles, as when Allan Ahlberg (cited in Moss 1990, p. 21) describes picturebooks as "an interweaving of word and pictures." The warp and woof of the loom are compared to the words and pictures "interweaving" with each other to produce a piece of cloth that would not exist if either warp or woof were missing. (Also see Curley's use of the word "interwoven" in the paragraph above.) Lewis (2001) points out that "the term *text*...is itself etymologically and semantically close to textile" (p. 33). This metaphor gestures toward the interdependence and interanimation that is discussed in the section on theoretical constructs.

Metaphors from Science and Technology

A few writers use metaphors from the disciplines of science and technology to describe the relationships between pictures and words. Moebius (1986) refers provocatively to the "plate tectonics" of the word–picture relationship. With this metaphor, Moebius is pointing out that, according to the theory that the surface of the earth is divided into a number of immense land masses that exist in a continually shifting relationship to each other, words and pictures in picturebooks can demonstrate various relationships within the same book. In addition, the metaphor suggests that words and pictures may "rub up" against each other, in uneasy and conflicting relationships, so that reader/viewers perceive the dynamic tensions that words and pictures sometimes manifest. Miller (1992) writes of the "interference" patterns between the visual and the verbal, referring to physics and wave theory. The theory suggests that two waves may combine with each other to form entirely new patterns. In the same way, words and pictures may be combined or integrated in the reader's mind to produce an entirely new interpretation or perspective on the narrative trajectory.

Curley (2007) compares the word–picture relationship to the Victorian invention called the stereopticon: "When focused, an image leaps from flatness into startling depth. It takes two camera lenses, set at slightly different angles, to create this magic. Now imagine an artist and a writer. Like the lenses of the stereopticon, they focus, from individual vantage points, on a narrative" (p. 7). In this metaphor, Curley emphasizes the different "vantage points" that words and pictures may take on a narrative, as well as the ability of the combination of words and pictures to create a more profound representation of literary reality as three-dimensional: more interesting, more complex, more nuanced.

Lewis (2001) provides a thought-provoking extended metaphor when he writes of the "ecology" of the picturebook. Just as all the animals and plants in a particular environment exist in a complex symbiosis with each other,

> …an ecological perspective on picturebooks tells us that words are never just words, they are always words-as-influenced-by-pictures. Similarly, the pictures are never just pictures, they are pictures-as-influenced-by-words. Thus, the words on their own are always partial, incomplete, unfinished, awaiting the flesh of the pictures. Similarly the pictures are perpetually pregnant with potential narrative meaning, indeterminate, unfinished, waiting the closure provided by the words (p. 74).

Lewis also rightly reminds us that the ecology of the picturebook means that the relationships between words and pictures can change from one double page spread to the next just as relationships are constantly changing in an ecosystem. So it's not that a picturebook can necessarily be categorized by a single text–picture relationship, regardless of the typology we utilize; rather, we must be on the lookout for shifts in this relationship as we examine the book. This is a point that needs to be kept in mind as we proceed into the next section on word–picture typologies. Lewis makes several other points about the ecological perspective—in a natural eco-system of a pond, for example, everything is related to everything else in a whole web of complex interdependence; likewise, this interdependence (a way of conceiving the book as an aesthetic whole) is one of the characteristics of a well-wrought picturebook. This extended metaphor is his chosen alternative to typologies, which he feels are ultimately unsuccessful in addressing the various types of text–picture relationships in picturebooks.

However, even though Lewis may have an excellent point, the analogical or comparative thinking metaphors utilize may be ultimately unsatisfying; metaphors, even extended ones like Lewis's, can only take us so far because the nature of metaphorical thinking is analogical, and ignores, for the moment, the many ways in which the metaphor is *not* at all like the phenomenon we are trying to describe. Therefore, writers have used theoretical constructs to more closely describe the relationship between words and pictures.

Theoretical Constructs

From this perspective, the relationship between words and pictures is explored through a number of theoretical constructs.

Irony

Nodelman (1988) and Kümmerling-Meibauer (1999) use the slippery concept of irony to partially explain the relation of words and pictures in picturebooks. Nodelman's perspective is that all texts and their accompanying pictures have the potential to be in an ironic relationship with one another. His argument is that, since the words tell us things that the pictures do not, and vice versa, the relationship is necessarily ironic. However, this depends on a very broad definition of irony, which Nodelman never actually makes explicit. As well, according to Kümmerling-Meibauer, there is no discernible irony in the relationship of words and pictures in many (perhaps most) picturebooks. Kümmerling-Meibauer, therefore, states that not all picturebooks have words and pictures that stand in ironic counterpoint to each other, but rather that the concept of irony is useful in some subcategory of picturebooks. She defines irony as

> fundamentally consist[ing] of a contrast between a spoken meaning and an implied, unspoken meaning. For this reason I will concentrate on the classical definition of irony (to say the opposite of what one means), since it represents the basic aspect of this literary trope that has to be learned by children (p. 160).

Kümmerling-Meibauer considers four different aspects/effects of the ironic relationship between text and pictures: (1) "semantic gap," in which there is important information missing from the text that is supplied by the pictures; (2) "contrast in artistic style," often exemplified by books in which the text is dull and mundane, but is accompanied by exuberant and humorous pictures; (3) "change in point of view," where the text presents a situation from one point of view (for example, the parents in Burningham's (1977) *Come Away from the Water, Shirley*) and the point of view of another character (Shirley and her unlimited imagination in the same book); and (4) "sequential structure," where the repetition and parallelism in incidents as the book proceeds help readers—even quite young readers—to perceive the ironic relationship between the text and pictures.

Another important point made by Kümmerling-Meibauer is that if we return to the definition of irony, we can understand that the double quality of irony is reflected in the double quality of the text and pictures:

> If one reconsiders the basic features of irony, which consist in a contrast between a spoken meaning ("said") and an implied, unspoken meaning ("unsaid"), and then draws a connecting line to the observation that the ironic content of the analyzed picture books lies in the complementarity between pictures and words, it would appear that, in this case, the text plays the part of the "said" and the picture exercises the function of the "unsaid," as it is in opposition to the text. The comparison between text as the spoken meaning and picture as the substitution for the implied but unspoken meaning should enable even preschool children to find pleasure in irony (p. 176).

See Agosto's typology below, in which she presents a slightly different definition of irony, which is used for two subcategories in her typology.

Limiting

Nodelman (1988) advances a useful construct he refers to as "limiting." Nodelman suggests that the words *limit* the pictures, just as the pictures simultaneously act to limit the words. For an example, Nodelman quotes the first sentence of *Snow White*. In the Randall Jarrell translation of the Grimm version, the words read, "At a window with a frame of ebony, a queen sat and sewed." The picture limits the words by showing us a particular window and a particular queen—not a generic one, but this specific window and this specific queen. In a sense, then, pictures limit the words by portraying one of many, many possible visual images that we might form in our minds. However, the words also limit the pictures. They do so because the words tell us what details are important and what details to pay attention to. Otherwise, the picture, with its multitude of details, might steer us off the track of the story. We might become fixated on the details of the queen's dress, or the background, or the chair in which she is sitting, etc. The point is that the words and pictures limit each other at the same time, but in different ways. There is an oscillation here that makes our minds go back and forth, in the process Barthes refers to as "relaying." Nodelman also makes use of Barthes's concept that the words "anchor" the illustrations, which perhaps suggested the idea of limiting to him.

Gesamtkunstwerk

Steiner (1988), writing about illustrated texts, refers to Wagner's concept of an opera as a "Gesamtkunstwerk" (an assembled or put-together work of art), with multimodalities interacting to produce the aesthetic whole of the opera. In opera, there are words, music, drama, movement, and visual aspects like costumes and stage sets. All these modalities are put together to produce the opera. In a similar way, Steiner comments that illustrated books (and by extension picturebooks), like opera, are "gesture[s] toward semiotic repletion, combining several kinds of sign types and having them comment on each other" (p. 144). In this way Steiner also harks back to the musical metaphors discussed above, as well as adding another metaphor, that of the words and pictures having a conversation, or "comment[ing] on each other." This idea of the Gesamtkunstwerk emphasizes the *simultaneity* of the modalities as they present themselves to our senses all at the same time, as well as the complex inter-relationships as the modalities affect one another dynamically and sequentially. The same dynamics operate in picturebooks.

Indeterminacies

Iser (1978), a reader-response theorist, writes that every literary text has gaps or "indeterminacies" which the reader is required to fill. Thus, readers play a very active role for Iser. Several writers comment that the words alone in picturebooks leave out certain information, and that the same is true for pictures, making Iser's theory useful to thinking about text–picture relationships. As Sendak (2007) comments, "You must never illustrate exactly what is written. You find a space in the text so that the pictures can do the work. Then you must let the words take over where words do it best." Graham (2000) echoes this when she states,

> …the creators of perfect picture books have recognized that the two media in which they work (words and pictures) need not, and often should not, 'say' the same thing. The discipline comes in being able to let each medium do what it does best and cutting away duplication (p. 61).

However, the real gap-filling is done in reader/viewers' minds as they use the words and pictures to fill in each others' indeterminacies. Kümmerling-Meibauer (1999) points out that another aspect of Iser's reader response theory, that of the reader's "wandering viewpoint," has an application to word–picture relationships. Iser argues that readers may place themselves in various relationships to a text; for example, at times, readers may identify with one character or another, or take the narrator's point of view. The application to text–picture relationships is that reader/viewers may at times take the point of view represented by the pictures, and at other times assume the point of view of the verbal text. This is perhaps most noticeable in picturebooks in which the text and pictures have an ironic relationship with each other (see above).

Synergy, Polysystemy, and Interanimation

Most of these theoretical constructs seem to have in common the idea that there is a way in which the totality of the picturebook, including words and pictures as well as peritextual elements, is much greater than the sum of its parts. Thus, my own term for the text–picture relationship is "synergy" defined as "the production of two or more agents, substances, etc., of a combined effect greater than the sum of their separate effects" (*Shorter Oxford English Dictionary*). In a picturebook, both the text and illustration sequence would be incomplete without the other. They have a synergistic relationship with each other in which the total effect depends not only on the "union" of text and illustrations but also on the perceived interactions or transactions between these two elements. In a very similar way, Lewis (2001) utilizes the term "polysystemy," "the piecing together of text out of different kinds of signifying systems." Lewis (2001) also expands convincingly Margaret Meek's (1991) idea that the words and pictures in picturebooks "interanimate" each other, and uses Nodelman's idea of the pictures limiting (see above) the text (by specifying what would otherwise be general and vague) and the text limiting the pictures (by pointing out what we should pay attention to in the multitude of possibilities in the picture). For Lewis, this is the way in which words and pictures interanimate each other, so that "A picturebook's 'story' is never to be found in the words alone, nor in the pictures, but emerges out of their mutual interanimation" (p. 36), a Gestaltist view that is quite similar to my idea of "synergy."

In general, all these theoretical constructs seem to get us a little closer to more precisely describing the complex relationships between words and pictures, but one thing is missing from all of them: they do not take into account the great *variations* in the ways the two sign systems relate to each other, instead substituting a generalized description. (See Nikolajeva and Scott, 2006, p. 8.) If we believe that words and pictures can relate to each other in many and various ways (often present in the same picturebook), we need to differentiate these ways; this leads us to typologies.

Typologies/Taxonomies

In *Ways of the Illustrator*, Joseph Schwarcz (1982) was perhaps the first to present an organized typology of word–picture relationships. Because the title of the section of his book is "Some Functions of the Illustration," we can conclude that he is primarily thinking of illustrations; however the section concerns the functions of pictures *as they relate to the words of the story*. He refers to "…this mutual game where words and pictures play together" (another metaphor for the text–picture relationship) (p. 14). I present this early typology in some detail, because (1) it seems to have been slightly misrepresented by some authors who write about text–picture relationships; and (2) it seems to have had a significant influence on subsequent typologies, both in terms of Schwarcz's general approach and his specific categories. He describes two main categories of these illustrational functions (as shown by the layout of major headings and subheadings of his text). In contrast, Nikolajeva and Scott (2006) do not seem to acknowledge that that there are two main categories with subcategories; they produce a simple list, which does not differentiate the two main categories from the subcategories; they also eliminate "Opposition/Alienation/Contradiction" (one of the subcategories of Deviation) from the list (see below).

Congruency

When the pictures confirm what the text says, then a congruency of the picture-text relationship contributes to the overall construction of the story. "[T]he pictures double or parallel what is said in the text," but "[t]here is never complete redundancy because the picture is more concrete than the word" (p. 14). Within this broad category, there are several functions:

Reduction The illustration simplifies or reduces the words, perhaps omitting background and action.
Elaboration On the other hand, the illustrations may elaborate what is said by the words; Schwarcz feels this is "one of the main functions of the illustration" (p. 15).
Amplification Closely related to elaboration, in this category, the illustration "temporarily stops the continuation of the main plot" (p. 15) by adding elements that might have happened prior to or after what is described in the words of the story.
Extension Here the illustration serves to add further interpretation to a simple statement. Schwarcz uses the example of a text stating that a girl did not answer a telephone, while the illustration shows that "she backed away from the phone and hid behind the window curtains" (p. 15).
Complementation For Schwarcz, this seems not to be a separate subcategory of congruency, but rather a combination of the four subcategories above: "In these examples, the illustrations complement what the text really means, as understood and interpreted by the illustrator" (p. 15).
Alternative progress In this form of congruency, the movement of the story proceeds by "text and pictures taking turns in continuing the story, with some of the steps in the plot presented only once, by either of the two" (p. 15). Here the classic example is the middle point of *Where the Wild Things Are* (Sendak, 1963), where the text stops and the pictures continue to depict the Wild Rumpus without any accompanying words.

Deviation

This is the opposite of Congruency, because in this case, the illustrator is inspired to "veer away" from the text "due to the illustrators's own associations and ideas" (p. 16). For Schwarcz, this deviation may happen in two different ways:

Opposition/Alienation/Contradiction In some cases, the illustration engages in "spiting, and thus spicing, the text" (p. 16). Schwarcz gives an example from a book illustrated by Toni Ungerer, where the text describes ducks swimming calmly in the water, whereas Ungerer's illustration depicts an artist painting a picture of a stork as well as a sly (and perhaps cruel) boy feeding ducks with the contents of a painter's paint tubes, which look like worms to the ducks. Even more contradictory to the text, the ducks are on land, not in the water.
Counterpoint In this last type of Deviation, text and illustrations tell two different (though related) stories. Schwarcz's example is *Rosie's Walk*

(Hutchins, 1971), in which the text is rather dull and uneventful, starkly recounting a hen's stroll around a barnyard, whereas the illustrations show an imminent danger to which the hen is oblivious: a fox, who is intent on capturing Rosie (and presumably eating her), but who is foiled in every double spread. Here Schwarcz explains in a very specific way the musical metaphor of counterpoint described above. "The technique of combining two or more melodic lines in such a way that they establish a harmonic relationship while retaining their linear individuality," in Schwarcz's interpretation, emphasizes the "linear individuality" of text and pictures—they tell "two entirely separate stories" (p. 17), while at the same time being paradoxically interdependent upon each other for reader/viewers' total meaning making, but not exactly in a harmonic relationship with each other.

Since "counterpoint" is used in other typologies, I want to make clear that there are at least two different ways of interpreting *Rosie's Walk*, which seems to be a very popular text for scholars to use in their typologies. On the one hand, following Schwarcz, we could say that the text and illustrations tell two different, though related, stories. On the other hand, we could say that the text and illustrations tell the same stories but through two different perspectives (in this case, the words from Rosie's perspective, and the pictures from the fox's perspective). Thus the term "counterpoint" proves to be rather slippery in its definition, and therefore its use in other typologies needs to be examined and explicated.

Golden (1990) has advanced a typology of word–picture relationships with five parts: (1) text and picture are symmetrical; (2) text depends on picture for clarification; (3) illustration enhances, elaborates text; (4) text carries primary narrative, illustration is selective; and (5) illustration carries primary narrative, text is selective. These categories seem to be differentiated by how much "work" the illustrations or the text do in conveying meaning. However, Golden's scheme is problematic. She asserts that, in category 1, the illustrations are redundant, only to admit later that there is no such thing as true redundancy. This tends to collapse category 1 with category 3. Then, too, what is the difference between the text depending on the picture for clarification (category 2) and the illustration enhancing or elaborating the text (category 3)? Although we would not expect rigid categories, these seem almost too blurred to be useful. In addition, the typology seems based almost solely on the relative amounts of *power* the text and illustrations have, thereby turning the word–picture relationship into a zero-sum game, where more influence by the pictures automatically means less influence by the words, and vice versa. The problem with this is that the relationship is not so much a matter of the balance of power as it is in the way in which the text and pictures transact with each other and transform each other; thus Golden's scheme tends to ignore the joint influence of words and pictures, and ends up discussing their relationship along only one dimension. Lewis (2001) also rightly critiques Golden's typology by being mostly focused on the text and the amount of text in proportion to the illustrations.

Here, Sipe intended to move on to discuss Barthes' notions of anchorage, illustration, and relaying (citation unspecified) and also Martinec and Salway (citation unspecified but probably 2005), as well as the work of Bodmer (1992) and Fang (1996), who "both advance ideas that might lead to taxonomies, but do not fully develop them."

Agosto (1999) begins her article on a typology of text–picture relationships in "interdependent storytelling" with this paragraph (footnotes are omitted):

> In most picture storybooks, the stories are told twice, once through text and once through illustration. The reader can comprehend such stories either through the words or through the pictures. Vandergrift called these books "twice-told tales" (68). Since both the texts and the illustrations of twice-told tales tell the same stories simultaneously, they employ *parallel storytelling*. Conversely, there exists a subset of picture storybooks for which the reader must consider both forms of media concurrently in order to comprehend the books' stories. Books belonging to this category employ *interdependent storytelling* (p. 267).

This introductory paragraph is problematic. In the opinion of most scholars, picturebooks are never simply "twice-told tales" because there is never complete redundancy between words and pictures, and because of the profound differences in these two sign systems (for the example, the visual sign system has a simultaneous orientation and presents space predominantly, and the verbal sign system has a sequential orientation and presents time predominantly). Even if twice-told tales were possible, they would be very poor picturebooks indeed: to what purpose or benefit? Agosto claims this situation is the case in "*most* picture storybooks" [italics mine] so for the select few picturebooks that employ "interdependent storytelling," Agosto advances a typology that also has several puzzling aspects.

Like Schwarcz's typology, Agosto's contains two main categories with subcategories for each. Her two main categories, "Augmentation" and "Contradiction," seem quite similar to Schwarcz's two main categories of "Congruency" and "Deviation."

Augmentation

Her first main category of Augmentation applies to situations where "the texts and the illustrations each amplify, extend, and complete the story that the other tells" (pp. 269–270). According to Agosto, Augmentation has the following five subcategories:

Irony Agosto follows Jon Stott's definition of irony: "discrepancy: between expectation and result, appearance and reality, statement and meaning, delusion and understanding" so that "a reader is expected to perceive discrepancies that are not clearly stated" (Stott, 1982, pp. 153–154)

Humor Here Agosto uses the example of Peggy Rathman's *Officer Buckle and Gloria* (1995), suggesting that the text makes sense when read alone, but the humor of the book is missing without the illustrations. However, the real humor of the book lies in the fact that Officer Buckle is oblivious to what Gloria (his police dog) is doing behind his back. We, the readers, know what is going on; in other words, there is a discrepancy between what we know and what Officer Buckle knows, so this example is confusing: it suggests that it is actually an example of irony, according to Agosto's definition, so that the first two subcategories of Augmentation may be conflated. Indeed, irony in picturebooks is frequently humorous. The distinction does not seem to be valid

Intimation In this category, the illustration "adds clues to the story," so that "the text without the pictures is incomplete" (p. 271). However, this is the case with almost all good picturebooks; the illustrations show us things that the words do not tell, and the words tell us things that the illustrations do not show. Thus, this subcategory seems to be applicable to almost all picturebooks and is therefore not particularly useful as one element in a typology

Fantastic representation In this subcategory, "the interdependent storytelling allows the reader to differentiate between fantasy and reality" (p. 272), as in the Shirley books by John Burningham. However, these books are surely prime examples of counterpoint and/or contradiction. Since "Contradiction" (see below) is Agosto's second *main* category, this subcategory—a subcategory of "Augmentation," seems out of place. The Shirley books could also be considered examples of irony, humor, and intimation, blurring the distinction among the subcategories

Transformation In this subcategory, "either the text or the illustration adds a deeper meaning to the story that is told primarily through the other of the two media forms" (p. 272). In adding this deeper meaning, the story is changed into a "radically different tale" (p. 273). However, how does this idea differ in essence from irony, humor, and intimation, the three other subcategories of Augmentation? To return to *Officer Buckle and Gloria*, surely the addition of the illustrations to the text in Rathman's picturebook makes it a "radically different tale," so "transformation" blurs into irony, as irony blurs into humor, intimation, and fantastic transformation, leaving us with more puzzles than clear delineations

Contradiction

Agosto's second main category is "Contradiction," which occurs when "the texts and illustrations present conflicting information, such as the words describing a sunny day where the corresponding pictures show a rainstorm" (p. 275).

Irony Here we are confronted with a subcategory that seems so similar to the subcategory of "irony" under the first main category of Augmentation that the attempt to differentiate them seems more confusing than convincing. Agosto seems to use the same definition of irony as in the subcategory under Augmentation, thereby conflating the two subcategories.

Humor Here, again, we have a subcategory that is given the same label as the second subcategory under the *first* main category of Augmentation. And similarly to the first two subcategories in the Augmentation, the example in Irony is humorous, so these two subcategories in Contradiction seem to be conflated.

Disclosure In this subcategory, the text–picture relationship "allows readers to know something the protagonist does not know" (p. 276). However, to return a third time to *Officer Buckle and Gloria*, the situation of readers knowing something the protagonist does not know is exactly the case in this picturebook, which is used as an example of "humor," the second subcategory of Augmentation. Thus, the entire typology seems to conflate itself to the two major categories, leaving the subcategories vague and blurry. Finally, Agosto's whole premise seems to be mainly concerned with the "added" effect of illustrations to text, rather than the equal effect of text on illustrations (and vice versa), and so has the opposite orientation from Golden's typology, which seems to be more text-centered. If texts and pictures are equally important, both typologies can be critiqued for this reason.

Here, Sipe intended to reference Lewis's (2001) critique of Agosto's typology, which makes some of the same points, and Lewis' application of Kress and van Leeuwen (1996) to picturebooks.

One of the most useful typologies is Nikolajeva and Scott's, which is presented partially in their article (2000) and more completely in their book (2006). They wisely discuss their typology as a continuum of word–picture relationships, and emphasize that some of the categories may blur or slide into each other. After discussing wordless (or almost wordless) picturebooks, and "narrative text with occasional illustrations"—at the extreme ends of the continuum—they proceed to discuss picture storybooks that fall between these two extremes. There are five major points along their continuum: (1) symmetrical picturebooks, which have "two mutually redundant narratives;" (2) complementary picturebooks, where "words and pictures have the function of 'filling each other's gaps;'" (3) "expanding" or "enhancing" picturebooks, where the "visual narrative supports verbal narrative" or "verbal narrative depends on visual narrative;" (4) "counterpointing" picturebooks, with "two mutually dependent narratives;" and (5) "sylleptic" picturebooks "with or without words," where "two or more narratives [are] independent of each other" (p. 12).

The first point on the continuum, symmetrical pictures, invites the question of whether the narrative provided by the words and that provided by the pictures can ever be truly "mutually redundant." The verbal and visual sign systems tell their stories in such different ways that the redundancy is questionable. I would suggest that there is never complete symmetry in the sense that the words simply reflect, as in a mirror, what the picture sequence shows us, or that the picture sequence simply reflects what the verbal narrative tells us. However, in some picturebooks, very little is added to the verbal narrative by the picture sequence. The picture sequence may add visual pleasure, but relatively little information.

The second point on the continuum (complementary picturebooks) seems to be derived mainly from Iser's idea of indeterminacies or gap-filling. Iser, of course, is thinking of novels, not picturebooks, but there is an appropriate application of this Iserian idea to picturebooks, so that words and pictures may be said to fill in each other's gaps.

The third point on the continuum, expanding or enhancing picturebooks, seems quite close to complementary picturebooks, because expanding or enhancing may be considered as a type of "gap-filling," which is the main point of complementary picturebooks.

The fourth point on the continuum, counterpointing picturebooks, consists of picturebooks that are "especially stimulating because they elicit many possible interpretations and involve the reader's imagination." Counterpointing is quite usefully expanded by Nikolajeva and Scott's (2006) insightful analysis of the various *types* of counterpointing that exist: (1) counterpoint *in address*, in which children and adults may fill in both textual and visual gaps in different ways (this speaks to the dual audience of picturebooks and literature for children in general). (2) counterpoint *in style*, where "words can be ironic while pictures are nonironic, or the other way around" (p. 24). As well, words and pictures may be serious/humorous; romantic/realistic, realistic/naive, historical/anachronistic, "artistic/popular; or other binaries." (3) counterpoint *in genre or modality*: words may be realistic while the illustrations are in the realm of fantasy (or vice versa): "While the verbal story is often told from a child's point of view, presenting the events as 'true,' the details in pictures suggest that the story takes place only in the child's imagination" (p. 24). (4) counterpoint *by juxtaposition*, which is the case in sylleptic picturebooks, where there are two or more parallel visual stories, "either supported or unsupported by words" (p. 25). (5) counterpoint *in perspective* (or point of view), the person who is seeing may be different from the person who is speaking, thereby representing at least two different perspectives on the same event or series of events. (6) counterpoint *in characterization*, in which "words and images can present characters in different and contradictory manners, thus creating irony and/or ambiguity" (p. 25). Either words or pictures may describe or show different sets of characters. (7) counterpoint *of metafictive nature*. (h) counterpoint *in space and time*, since pictures are best at presenting space, while words are best at presenting the passage of time (though this is not a rigid distinction, and both words and pictures have ways of presenting both space and the passage of time).

In fact, the whole of Nikolajeva and Scott's book "explore[s] the variety of text–image interactions in picturebooks," using the above categories "to shape [their] discussion" (p. 26).

Marsh and White's (2003) taxonomy of 3 major categories with 49 subcategories in all, was developed by examining a variety of taxonomies already published and doing a qualitative content analysis of almost a thousand text–image pairs. They claim their taxonomy is applicable to all text types (and by implication to picturebooks), and cite Nikolajeva and Scott's (2006) book in addition to several articles specifically about picturebooks, including Bodmer (1992) and Fang (1996). There are many subcategories based on these picturebook scholars.

In terms of usefulness, the various typological models of word–picture relationships emphasize the variety and complexity of these relationships. Some scholars, such as Lewis (2001) are wary of any typologies, no matter how complex, because the world of picturebooks may exemplify an almost limitless variety. There is, however, another important dimension to this question, one that emphasizes what goes on in reader/viewers' minds as they explore a picturebook, that necessitates consideration of various phenomenological approaches.

Transmediation: Phenomenological Descriptions

Unfortunately, this section, which would have included discussion of much of Sipe's own work, was only sketched out. Here we present references named by Sipe in his planning notes and, in some cases, notes on those sources.

Bortolussi and Dixon (2003).
Paivio and Csapo, 1973: Dual coding hypotheses: image and verbal memory codes are independent and additive in their effect on recall. In addition, the contribution of imagery appeared to be substantially higher than that of the verbal code. Thus the usual superiority of pictures in free recall is best explained by dual encoding, or a combination of image superiority and dual coding, both of which are ordinarily favored when items are presented as pictures. [See Wikipedia for a brief description of this theory, plus some bibliographic citations]. It also supports Roman Jakobson's (1985) assertion that the visual always trumps the verbal in importance in the reader/viewer's mind. Sipe may have meant Verbal Art, Verbal Sign, Verbal Time.

Spatial and temporal arts/simultaneity and linearity (Lessing, no citation noted)
Tension between lingering on the pictures and dashing ahead with the words (Doonan, 1983).
Semiotically framed theories including my own.

The following were not specified, but were taken from his vita.

Sipe, Lawrence R. (1998). How Picturebooks Work: A Semiotically Framed Theory of Text–Picture Relationships. *Children's Literature in Education, 29(2)*, 97–108.

Sipe, Lawrence R. (2001). Picturebooks as Aesthetic Objects. *Literacy Teaching and Learning: An International Journal of Early Reading and Writing, 6*, 23–42.

Sipe, Lawrence R. (2008a). *Storytime: Young Children's Literary Understanding in the Classroom*. New York: Teachers College.

Sipe, Lawrence R. (2008b). Young Children's Visual Meaning-Making in Response to Picturebooks. In James Flood, Shirley Brice-Heath, & Diane Lapp (Eds.), *Handbook of Research in Teaching Literacy Through the Visual and Communicative Arts* (Vol. II, pp. 381–392). New York: Lawrence Erlbaum.

Sipe, Lawrence R. (2010). The Art of the Picturebook. In Shelby A. Wolf, Karen Coats, Patricia Enciso, & C. Jenkins (Eds.), *Handbook of Research in Children's and Young Adult Literature* (pp. 238–252). New York: Routledge.

References

Picture Storybooks

Burningham, John. (1977). *Come Away from the Water, Shirley*. New York: Red Fox.
Hutchins, Pat. (1971). *Rosie's Walk*. New York: Simon & Schuster.
Rathman, Peggy. (1995). *Officer Buckle and Gloria*. New York: Penguin.
Sendak, Maurice. (1963). *Where the Wild Things are*. New York: Harper Collins.

Theory and Criticism

Agosto, Denise.E. (1999). One and Inseparable: Interdependent Storytelling in Picture Storybooks. *Children's Literature in Education, 30*(4), 267–280.
Barthes, Roland. (1978). *Image-Music-Text* (S. Heath, Trans.). New York: Hill and Wang.
Bodmer, George R. (1992). Appreciating the Illustrated Text. In Glen E. Sadler (Ed.), *Teaching Children's Literature: Issues, Pedagogy, Resources*. New York: Modern Language Association.
Bortolussi, Marissa, & Dixon, Peter. (2003). *Psychonarratology: Foundations for the Empirical Study of Literary Response*. Cambridge: Cambridge University press.
Cech, Jon. (1983). Remembering Caldecott: 'The Three Jovial Huntsmen' and the Art of the Picturebook. *The Lion and the Unicorn, 84*(7/89), 110–119.
Curley, J.B. (2007). Children Should be Seen: A Curatorial Overview. In Curated by Leonard S. Marcus, Jane Bayard Curley, & Caroline Ward, *Children Should be Seen: The Image of the Child in American Picture-Book Art*. Amherst, MA: The Katonah Museum of Art and the Eric Carle Museum of Picture Book Art.
Curley, J., & Burkert, N.E. (2003). *Nancy Ekholm Burkert: The Art of Illustration: A Deep and Delicate Vision*. Amherst, MA: The Eric Carle Museum of Picture Book Art.
Doonan, Jane. (1983). *Looking at Pictures in Picture Books*. Exeter: Thimble Press.
Eisner, Elliot W. (1979, 1985, 1994). *The Educational Imagination: On the Design and Evaluation of School Programs*. New York: Macmillan.
Fang, Z. (1996). Illustrations, Text and the Child Reader: What are Pictures in Children's Storybooks for? *Reading Horizons, 37*(2), 130–142.
Golden, Joanne M. (1990). *The Narrative Symbol in Childhood Literature: Explorations in the Construction of Text*. Berlin: Mouton.
Graham, Judith. (2000). Creativity and Picture Books. *Literacy, 34*(2), 61–67.
Iser, Wolfgang. (1978). *The Act of Reading: A Theory of Aesthetic Response*. Baltimore: Johns Hopkins.
Jakobson, Roman. (1985). *Verbal Art, Verbal Sign, Verbal Time*. Minneapolis: University of Minnesota Press.
Kress, Gunther, & Van Leeuwen, Theo. (1996). *Reading Images: The Grammar of Visual Design*. London: Routledge.
Kümmerling-Meibauer, Bettina. (1999). Metalinguistic Awareness and the Child's Developing Concept of Irony: The Relationship Between Pictures and Text in Ironic Picturebooks. *The Lion and the Unicorn, 23*, 157–183.
Lanes, Selma. (1980). *The Art of Maurice Sendak*. New York: Abrams.
Lewis, David. (2001). *Reading Contemporary Picturebooks: Picturing Text*. New York: Routledge/Falmer.
Marsh, E.E., & White, M.D. (2003). A Taxonomy of Relationships Between Images and Texts. *Journal of Documentation, 59*(6), 647–672.
Massey, Irving. (1980). Words and Images: Harmony and Dissonance. *Georgia Review, XXXIV*, 375–395.
Martinec, R., & Salway, A. (2005). A System for Image–Text Relations in New (and Old) Media. *Visual Communication, 4*(3), 337–371.
Meek, Margaret. (1991). *On Being Literate*. London: The Bodley Head.
Miller, J.H. (1992). *Illustration*. Cambridge, MA: Harvard University Press.
Moebius, William. (1986). Introduction to Picturebook Codes. *Word and Image, 2*, 141–158.
Moss, Joy. (1990). *Focus on Literature: A Context for Literacy Learning*. Katonah, NY: Owen.
Nikolajeva, Maria, & Scott, Carole. (2000). The Dynamics of Picturebook Communication. *Children's Literature in Education, 31*(4), 225–239.
Nikolajeva, Maria, & Scott, Carole. (2006). *How Picturebooks Work*. New York: Routledge.
Nodelman, Perry. (1988). *Words About Pictures: The Narrative Art of Children's Picturebooks*. Athens, GA: University of Georgia Press.
Paivio, A., & Csapo, K. (1973). Picture Superiority in Free Recall: Imagery or Dual Coding? *Cognitive Psychology, 5*, 176–206.
Pullman, Philip. (1989). Invisible Pictures. *Signal, 60*, 160–186.
Schwarcz, Joseph H. (1982). *Ways of the Illustrator: Visual Communication in Children's Literature*. Chicago: American Library Association.
Sendak, Maurice. (1984). Introduction. In J. Cott (Ed.), *Victorian Color Picture Books*. New York: Allen Lane/Stonehill/Chesea House.

Sendak, Maurice. (2007). In P.L. Gauch, D. Briggs, C. Palmer, & K. Steurer (Eds.), *Artist to Artist: 23 Major Illustrators Talk to Children About Their Art* (p. 74). New York: Philomel.
Sipe, Lawrence R. (1998). How Picturebooks Work: A Semiotically Framed Theory of Text–Picture Relationships. *Children's Literature in Education, 29*(2), 97–108.
Sipe, Lawrence R. (2001). Picturebooks as Aesthetic Objects. *Literacy Teaching and Learning: An International Journal of Early Reading and Writing, 6*, 23–42.
Sipe, Lawrence R. (2008a). *Storytime: Young Children's Literary Understanding in the Classroom*. New York: Teachers College.
Sipe, Lawrence R. (2008b). Young Children's Visual Meaning-Making in Response to Picturebooks. In James Flood, Shirley Brice-Heath, & Diane Lapp (Eds.), *Handbook of Research in Teaching Literacy Through the Visual and Communicative Arts* (Vol. II, pp. 381–392). New York:Lawrence Erlbaum.
Sipe, Lawrence R. (2010). The Art of the Picturebook. In Shelby A. Wolf, Karen Coats, Patricia Enciso, & C. Jenkins (Eds.), *Handbook of Research in Children's and Young Adult Literature* (pp. 238–252). New York: Routledge.
Spaulding, Amy E. (1995). *The Page as a Stage Set: Storyboard Picture Books*. Metuchen, NJ: Scarecrow Press.
Steiner, W. (1988). *The Colors of Rhetoric*. Chicago: The University of Chicago Press.
Stott, Jon. (1982). It's Not What You Expect: Teaching Irony to Third Graders. *Children's Literature in Education, 13*, 153–163.
Ward, John L., & Fox, Marian Nitti. (1984). A Look at Some Outstanding Illustrated Books for Children. *Children's Literature Association Quarterly, 9*(1), 19–21.
Wiesner, David. (2010). Points of Departure. In S.A. Wolf, K. Coats, P. Enciso, & C.A. Jenkins (Eds.), *Handbook of Research in Children's and Young Adult Literature* (pp. 254–255). New York: Routledge.
Wyile, A. (2006). The Drama of Potentiality in Metafictive Picturebooks: Engaging Pictorialization in Shortcut, Ooh-la-la, and Voices in the Park (with Occasional Assistance from A. Wolf's True Story). *Children's Literature Association Quarterly, 31*(2), 176–196.

Children's Literature in Education (2012) 43:22–26
DOI 10.1007/s10583-011-9151-2

COMMEMORATIVE ISSUE FOR DR. LAWRENCE SIPE

Children's Literature *and* Education: A Memoir of Dr. Lawrence Sipe

Rachel Skrlac Lo

Published online: 15 February 2012
© Springer Science+Business Media, LLC 2012

Abstract A personal reflection about Dr. Sipe as a teacher and a mentor.

Keywords Dr. Sipe · Tribute · Memorial · Reflections

"Knowing you, dear Gower, has been one of the most rewarding experiences of my life," said Abel. (Steig, 1976, p. 94)

This issue marks the one-year anniversary of Dr. Lawrence Sipe's untimely death. While he was a renowned scholar in the field of children's literature in education, he also was a phenomenal educator. For 15 years he taught educators, researchers, and scholars about the power of children's literature. He took great joy in this position and often marveled at his good fortune to teach only classes that focused on this literature. Dr. Sipe's office reflected his passion, with books bursting off of bookshelves, often stacked two deep! His personal library of books—including picturebooks, academic texts, and novels for young adults—contained nearly 5,000 titles. While the walls may have moaned and strained from the weight of his library, the spirit that emanated from his office resonated with joy, wonder and laughter.

Intertwined among the scholarly articles in this journal to honor Dr. Sipe's work are a series of reflections from some of his former students. Each of us had a unique

---

Rachel Skrlac Lo is a Ph.D. student in the Reading/Writing/Literacy program at the University of Pennsylvania's Graduate School of Education. Her research focus is on gender identity formation and early literacy experiences, and she has a particular interest in picturebooks and educational media. Rachel was Dr. Sipe's graduate assistant for 2010/2011, which included the role of editorial assistant for *Children's Literature in Education*.

R. S. Lo (✉)
Reading/Writing/Literacy, Graduate School of Education, University of Pennsylvania, 3700 Walnut Street, Philadelphia, PA 19104, USA
e-mail: skrr@gse.upenn.edu

 Springer

Reprinted from the journal

relationship with him; our diverse connections reveal the scope of his knowledge and interests. These memories are but a small sampling of the tributes to Dr. Sipe. Ours are no better or more important. Their inclusion in this journal is the result of a desire to allow this memorial issue to reflect *beyond* his scholarly impact on the field. For, while Dr. Sipe was a significant scholar and researcher, he was also a tender and meticulous teacher. His presence in the classroom, in his office, and on the University of Pennsylvania campus is greatly missed.

We are united in our grief for Dr. Sipe's passing and for the subsequent changes to our academic community, a community that was made richer because of his passion for children's literature, his devotion to understanding childhood reading experiences, and especially his delight in teaching people about his discoveries and ideas. His enthusiasm resonated with each of us and inspired us to push at our own boundaries. While Dr. Sipe's spirit lives on in the work each of us does, still we miss him every day and wonder how our academic careers—which we are just beginning—have been altered because of his premature passing. For us, his death marks the loss of a great teacher, mentor, and scholar who had much to share, which he did so generously.

I had the good fortune of taking Dr. Sipe's class, Responding to Literature, a required course for doctoral students, during my first semester at Penn. Through this class we explored literacy theories and each class was grounded in one or two books from Dr. Sipe's library. In the first class he read aloud *The Faithful Elephants* (1997), written by Yukio Tsuchiya and illustrated by Ted Lewin, a picturebook based on the true story of the fate of the elephants housed at the Ueno Zoo in Tokyo during World War II. It is a terribly sad story and by the end of the book there wasn't a dry eye in the room. Even Dr. Sipe had to pause several times to recompose himself, though he read it aloud in this class every year.

Dr. Sipe's decision to read a tragic tale to us was purposeful. He wanted this room full of rather learned people to feel the power of a picturebook, to understand that picturebooks are more than "cute kiddie lit" (a phrase he despised). In the conversation that followed, we discussed the issues around international perspectives of World War II, metaphors for human experiences, symbolism, the meaning of peritextual design elements in the book, and much more. Each week, as in this first class, Dr. Sipe would anchor theory to different literary experiences, welcoming all comments—often looking down at his tie to encourage a democratic space for discussion—and he would draw on his vast wealth of knowledge to help us construct meaning and understanding.

And so, while Dr. Sipe was indeed a brilliant scholar, he also was a powerful voice in the university classroom, and he loved his students. Many weeks, he would proudly announce that a former student had authored our required reading, and he would discuss strategic tips for getting published in academic journals. He was beloved for many, many reasons, especially because he brought to our academic experience a playful joy of learning, an opportunity to look at our own childhood memories and understand them from a different perspective, and an appreciation for children's literature as a valuable source for understanding societies, teaching practices, and ourselves.

My Tale: *Fabula and Syuzhet*

...the main purpose of literature is to allow us to acutely experience the freshness and vibrancy of life, through literary techniques and practices that 'defamiliarize' life and make it strange and new again. (Sipe, 2008, p. 48)

This quote, and the terms *fabula* and *syuzhet*, echo throughout my memories of Dr. Sipe. Perhaps it is because he introduced these terms and Shklovsky's work as a Russian formalist to my academic repertoire, perhaps because I still wrestle with exactly what they mean, or perhaps it is the visual memory of him and his joyful demeanor when using these terms. My memories of Dr. Sipe are a part of the story of how I became a doctoral student. From the first time I heard his name to the first time I met him to the last time I saw him and the last email I got from him, I can lay these memories out end-to-end. This is my story of Dr. Sipe, a series of linear events that occur in real time (Sipe, 2008), or the *fabula* of a relationship; but for many of you, the readers, my story of Dr. Sipe is only a small part of your knowledge of him. I hope that I can shape my story and create *syuzhet* that resonates and informs you, and that my memories can be integrated into your own, thus deepening the plot of who Larry Sipe was. For it is not just literature that can instruct and delight us, but people, and Dr. Sipe, in his own passion for children's literature and children's engagement with literature, not only did this, but did it in such a way that he fulfilled his own expectations for literature: he defamiliarized the 'life' of children's literature, filling it with vibrancy and life for all of us.

My own experience with Dr. Sipe was very privileged. He was my advisor and I was his graduate assistant. But our relationship wasn't as simple as that. For me, a mother of two young children returning to full-time study after 7 years as a stay-at-home parent, the transition to graduate school was emotional, intense, and in many ways all-consuming. Dr. Sipe opened a door to the Academy that was supportive and encouraging. As others will attest, his door was open to everyone, but I had the good fortune to have weekly meetings with him. We would talk about research projects and the work that needed to be done for this journal and his courses, but he always had time to check in on my "growing pains" as I learned to juggle my family's needs aside my newly acquired academic ones. His laughter at my wry humor, often followed with the chuckling phrase, "You have such a great sense of humor, Rachel! Don't ever lose it!" gave me space to relax in his company, to consider him someone who would be a stalwart support for me as I progressed through the doctoral program.

This support was confirmed in June when, 3 months after his death, I received an email from Alexis Wolson, an Assistant Dean at GSE. I had received an award to fund my studies on early childhood literacy. When I asked how I was selected for this award, I discovered that Dr. Sipe had recommended me for the award the previous December. The thrill of receiving the award was that much sweeter because of this special connection to Dr. Sipe, but it was also poignant since it reminded me of my own personal loss.

During my first semester at Penn, starting in September 2010, I often marveled—truly!—at the consequence of serendipity that I was working with someone as knowledgeable and well-respected as Dr. Sipe, and to have this incredible opportunity to be surrounded by picturebooks on a daily basis—picturebooks I could immerse myself in and use to carve out a scholarly career. He understood my marveling and, often while working together in his office, we would acknowledge, with a slight giddiness, our fortuitous luck to be able to devote our careers to studying children's literature, and in an Ivy League institution no less!

One very special memory of Dr. Sipe is from last February, only a few weeks before he passed away. We were discussing a submission to this journal and were debating whether the results supported the argument presented. Cited children's books were flying off the shelves as we studied the work of different illustrators. This was not a heated debate but scholarly inquiry as we worked together to ensure the submission's authors were consistent. In the midst of a fine-combed analysis of a book by David Wiesner, Holly Link, a doctoral student from the Educational Linguistics program, knocked on the door. She said, "I'm sorry to bother you, but I just wanted to let you know how much I enjoy listening to your conversations." She worked in the cubicle outside his office and was able to hear our regular conversations. Then she left, leaving us to our inquiry. This was the last article I worked on with Dr. Sipe, and it was one that he approved just before he passed away. It holds a special place in my heart because it is a very good article and because it represents a significant moment in my own academic work. When I learned that Dr. Sipe had passed away, one of my first thoughts was that I would never have another day like that one to share with him.

I still have many days when I think about Dr. Sipe and about the few months I had with him as his graduate assistant. His door was always open, and so was his heart. My last meeting with him was the day before I left for a family vacation over spring break. Dr. Sipe and I were finalizing plans to revise two chapters of the 8th edition of *Literature and the Child*, a textbook he co-authored with Lee Galda. I was working at a table outside his office and he came to me several times over the course of an afternoon to ask me questions about the project. Each time, he was so gracious. I remember thinking that his gratitude was not necessary, I was his graduate assistant and this is what graduate assistants do. I was excited about the project and had packed materials from the textbook to work on during my vacation. Before I left, he came out of his office and said to me again, "Thank you. Thank you for everything you do for me." I remember thinking that he seemed tired, but I also know he was excited about all the work we had to do. I did not think for a minute that these words would be the last words we would ever share.

This past July, I helped dismantle and pack up Dr. Sipe's library. I wanted to be a part of this process, to be able to say goodbye to him by ensuring his belongings were organized and sorted just the way he would want them sorted. Four of us, including his sister Judy, worked through the hottest week of the summer to catalogue his books, to sort his files, and to put the final effects of his life in order. I had expected this to be an act of closure for me, a point when the grief would recede, but in those long, hot, humid hours, I found my grief mounting as each box was sealed. In the end, I helped pack nearly 5,000 books. When I left his office, it was not Lawrence Sipe's office anymore. It was someone else's. I know this new professor has the right to make it his own space, to create an institutional identity that is his, but for me the space behind that door will always be bursting with picturebooks, full of the colorful emotions so vibrantly portrayed in the books and in the work Dr. Sipe did. I hope that I will be as true to my own academic voice as he was, and in doing so, I may—just maybe—be able to leave a trace of his legacy in my work.

References

Sipe, Lawrence R. (2008). *Storytime: Young Children's Literary Understanding in the Classroom*. New York: Teachers College Press.
Steig, William. (1976). *Abel's Island*. New York: Farrar, Strauss and Giroux.
Tsuchiya, Yukio. (1997). *The Faithful Elephants*. New York: Sandpiper.

Children's Literature in Education (2012) 43:27–47
DOI 10.1007/s10583-011-9158-8

COMMEMORATIVE ISSUE FOR DR. LAWRENCE SIPE

Navigating Worlds of "Trouble and Woe and Worse" in Children's Literature: An Exploration into the Double Text of Tony Kushner and Maurice Sendak's *Brundibar*

Kristin M. Larsen

Published online: 15 February 2012
© Springer Science+Business Media, LLC 2012

Abstract In this article, the author explores the richly layered double text of Kushner and Sendak's picturebook, *Brundibar* (2003)—the historical context of *Brundibár* as a Holocaust-era children's operetta by Hans Krása and Adolf Hoffmeister, and the present day manifestation of *Brundibar* as a children's picturebook. In order to contextualize the discussion of Kushner and Sendak's text, *Brundibar*'s historical origins in Nazi-annexed Czechoslovakia and its transition to the stage in the Nazi "model" concentration camp, Terezín, is presented. An extensive semiotic analysis of Kushner and Sendak's illustrations and text is also provided within the framework of what Kushner (*The art of Maurice Sendak: 1980 to the present*, 2003) terms "a world of trouble and woe and worse" (p. 210). Furthermore, the author discusses the development of Sendak's Hitlerian Brundibar and the struggles that both Kushner and Sendak faced as they considered how to portray the story's antagonist, given their somewhat differing conceptions of which difficult themes and topics children should be exposed to during childhood. To round out this

---

Kristin M. Larsen is a doctoral student in the Reading/Writing/Literacy program at the University of Pennsylvania's Graduate School of Education. Prior to beginning her doctoral studies, Kristin worked as a teacher of English language learners (ELLs) at the elementary and middle school levels, and as an ELL family literacy instructor and after-school German teacher. From 2006 to 2007, she served as an English as a Foreign Language Teaching Assistant with Austrian-American Educational Commission/Fulbright Commission in Salzburg, Austria. Kristin holds an M.Ed. in Curriculum and Instruction: Multilingual/ Multicultural Education from George Mason University and a B.A. in German Language & Literature and International Letters and Visual Studies from Tufts University. She is also a Teacher Consultant for the Northern Virginia Writing Project.

K. M. Larsen
University of Pennsylvania, Philadelphia, PA, USA

K. M. Larsen (✉)
University of Pennsylvania Graduate School of Education, 3700 Walnut Street,
Philadelphia, PA 19104-6216, USA
e-mail: krlarsen@gse.upenn.edu

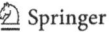

discussion, the author explores pedagogical implications for teachers as they read difficult texts, particularly Holocaust texts, with children.

Keywords Constructions of childhood · Holocaust · Difficult texts · Hitler · Brundibar · Semiotic analysis · Tony Kushner · Maurice Sendak · Bumble-Ardy

Foreword

I am endlessly indebted to the teaching and mentoring of my beloved professor, Dr. Lawrence Sipe (1949–2011), who introduced me to Kushner and Sendak's *Brundibar* when I was a student in his doctoral seminar, Responding to Literature, at the University of Pennsylvania's Graduate School of Education. It was Dr. Sipe's passion for this picturebook and its historical context that instantly inspired me to further explore it as a source of scholarly inquiry. I am grateful for Dr. Sipe's initial feedback, suggestions, and revisions on my first draft of this article, and I deeply regret that he will not see it in its published form.

Fear, Mortality, and the Holocaust as Muse: The Works of Maurice Sendak

For the past 50 years, Maurice Sendak has been a prolific and unparalleled writer and illustrator of children's picturebooks that have not only sparked the imagination of children and adults alike, but have wrestled with the *wild things* of the human condition. Born in Brooklyn to Polish–Jewish immigrant parents, Sendak was a sickly child who spent a good deal of his childhood indoors, watching the other children play outside from his window and sketching pictures of them in his notebook (Lanes, 1980). In a PBS interview with Moyers (2004), Sendak noted that he was aware of his own mortality from an early age:

> [My parents] always thought I was gonna die…My grandmother, sewed me a suit of white with white stockings and white shoes. And I would sit on the stoop in front of the house with her so that the angel of death would pass over…I would not be taken as long as I was dressed in white.

The entrancing, and often frightening, dreamscape-like quality of many of Sendak's works reflects his fears and acute awareness of his mortality. For example, Sendak has said that his childhood fear of his Eastern European Jewish relatives' visits inspired the monsters in *Where the Wild Things Are* (1963). In a 1989 speech at the University of Washington, he said, the wild things were his relatives "…only much more personable. I hated them all. They were grotesque, with their huge noses, their great cascades of hair, their bad teeth. Worse, they ate our food. I didn't understand why they had to spoil our Sundays" (Shirk, 1989, 1D). Sendak has also noted that his fear of being kidnapped like the Lindbergh baby, who was kidnapped in 1932, and the effect that seeing a photo of the baby's corpse prompted him to include a likeness of the dead baby in *Outside Over There* (1981) (Bangs and Jonze,

2010). As is quite evident in many of Sendak's works, Kushner (2003) noted that, "Sendak has never slept soundly, not even as a child" (p. 24).

Sendak's treatment of dark and difficult subjects is wholly apparent in what Kushner (2003) identifies as Sendak's trilogy, *Outside Over There*, *Dear Mili* (1988), and *We Are All in the Dumps with Jack and Guy* (1990), three books which portray children as agents of their own survival in worlds where they have been abandoned, and in the case of *Jack and Guy*, exploited by the very adults who should be caring for them.[1] When asked whether it is difficult for him to place children in jeopardy in his drawings, Sendak replied that he believes all children are in jeopardy: "I think it is unnatural to think that there is such a thing as a blue-sky, white-clouded happy childhood for anybody" (Inskeep, 2006). Challenging such saccharin images of childhood, Sendak's works have often dealt with the darker themes of childhood struggles and mortality.

In his latest picturebook, *Bumble-Ardy* (2011), Sendak again explores the possibility of a jeopardized childhood. Bumble-Ardy, a young, orphaned pig who was adopted by his Aunt Adeline, has never had a birthday party. For his ninth birthday, Bumble-Ardy secretly throws himself a raucous party while Aunt Adeline is at work. When she returns home to find Bumble-Ardy's friends guzzling her home-brewed brine, Aunt Adeline shuts down the party in a wild fury, and evokes the "never again" often associated with the Holocaust (Gross, 2011). Bumble-Ardy, in tears, replies, "I promise! I swear! I won't ever turn ten!" While *Bumble-Ardy* has a happy ending, we see a young child and an orphan of murdered parents who has had many of the happier moments of childhood either denied or deferred.

The depiction of what Pulitzer Prize-winning playwright, liberal activist and *Brundibar* author Tony Kushner (2003) calls "a world of trouble and woe and worse" (p. 210) is a less traversed and difficult topic to approach in modern children's literature, a genre that has largely "reproduced the dominant interpretation of the world [that] anticipated a happy ending" (Pape, 1992, p. 180). While *Outside Over There, Dear Mili, We're All in the Dumps with Jack and Guy*, and *Bumble-Ardy* are masterfully crafted picturebooks, they deal with issues that adults might find frightening to children. It is many adults' desire to construct childhood as a time of unadulterated innocence and "happily-ever-after endings" in a world of "trouble and woe and worse" that leads them to censor which stories children have access to. As adults make choices about which books and subject matter are appropriate for young readers, it has often been expressed that Sendak's work "is not universally suitable for all children, that it is too strong" and "too scary" (Kushner, 2003, p. 22).

However, as Sipe (1996) found in reading *Jack and Guy* with two young children, a first-grader and a second-grader, "What adults see in the book may well not be what children see" (p. 100). Furthermore, Sendak has made clear how he feels about adult censorship and persistent happy endings in children's literature. In *Caldecott & Co.* (1989), Sendak writes, "I don't think I'm stretching the point when I suggest that this 'let's-make-the-world-a-happy-easy-frustration-less-place-for-the-kids' attitude is

---

[1] In contrast with Kushner, Sendak has identified his trilogy as *Where the Wild Things Are* (1963), *In the Night Kitchen* (1970), and *Outside Over There* (1981).

often propounded in children's literature today...I believe there exists a quiet but highly effective adult censorship of subjects that are supposedly too frightening, or morbid, or not optimistic enough, for boys and girls" (p. 158).

Another Sendak work, *Brundibar*[2] (2003), is not part of what Kushner identifies as Sendak's trilogy, but could perhaps be considered a continuation and expansion of the themes explored in those texts. Sendak has noted that he considers *Brundibar* to be a work that has given him closure for the "lifelong cultural and personal traumas inflicted by the Holocaust" (Knoepflmacher, 2005, p. 173). Similarly, in an interview with NPR's Gross (2006), Sendak noted that *Brundibar* was a more deeply personal work for him than any of his works prior because of its direct link to the Holocaust, the memories of which he has carried around with him since his childhood. He recalled:

> There was no such thing as childhood... [I was] unhappily reminded endlessly of my good fortune, and if I came up late for dinner... I'd hear about Leo and Benjamin and the other children my age who could never come up for supper and were good to their mothers, but now they were dead, and I was lucky. You're in mourning all the time...I hated *them* for dying.

Re-Imagining *Brundibár:* Sendak and Kushner in Collaboration

After hearing a Czech-language recording of Brundibár shared with him by actor-director Bob Jaffe (Kushner, 2003, p. 205), Sendak asked his friend Tony Kushner, perhaps best known for his Pulitzer Prize-winning political drama *Angels in America: A Gay Fantasia on National Themes* (1995), to collaborate with him in adapting Brundibár into an English-language libretto and picturebook. In his Sendak chronicle, *The Art of Maurice Sendak: 1980 to the Present* (2003), Kushner admits that he has been a fan of Sendak's work since he was 4 years old and that Sendak has greatly influenced his own works (p. 7). Like Sendak, Kushner is also a Jewish-American who has dealt with the issues of fascism and the Holocaust in his plays and essays. Most notably, *A Bright Room Called Day* (1992) explores issues of past and current political engagement and controversially equates the rise of Adolf Hitler to the Reaganism of 1980's America. Considering Kushner's reverence for Sendak's works and children's literature in general, his concern with the heinous crimes of Nazi Germany being repeated, and the fact that some of his earliest plays were children's plays (Fisher, 2008, p. 101), it could be argued that Kushner was a perfect choice to collaborate with Sendak on bringing *Brundibár* to English-speaking audiences.

Tony Kushner and Maurice Sendak's collaboration resulted in the Czech, World War II-era children's operetta, composed by Hans Krása with a libretto written by Adolf Hoffmeister, being re-imagined as an English-language picturebook and stage performance. *Brundibar* is a home-away-home story reminiscent of the Grimm Brothers' *Märchen*, *Hansel and Gretel* (Knoepflmacher, 2005) that tells the tale of a

---

[2] Both Brundibár and *Brundibar* are used in this work. Brundibár denotes the Krása and Hoffmeister operetta, while *Brundibar* denotes Kushner and Sendak's picturebook and stage-adaptation.

child brother-sister pair, Pepicek and Aninku, and their struggle in the face of bullies to bring milk home to their sick mother. Bullying is a prominent theme in *Brundibar* and the narrative explores what happens to bullies when their victims unite and rise up against them. Following the thread of political activism evident in his prior works, Kushner (2006) writes that *Brundibar* is a story that should exhort us to action against the world's bullies and tyrants: "Be brave, and you can make bullies behave! Rely on friends! Make common cause, build communities, organize and resist!" (p. 13). While the story can be said to have a happy-ending, as the children eventually succeed in bringing home the much-needed milk to their ailing mother, Kushner (2003) remarks, "It's a sweet tale, but it has a tragic history" (p. 206).

Brundibar's history is tragic, indeed, as it is both product and victim of the Holocaust-era, a time when no Jewish man, woman, or child was safe from the horrors of the Nazi concentration camps. This is the history that makes *Brundibar* such a difficult tale to tell children, and it caused Sendak and Kushner to struggle with just how to approach their telling of it. Kushner (2003) writes that their discussions surrounding the treatment of the story raised the following questions:

> In a world of trouble and woe and worse, what are children to be told? How much knowledge should they be spared? How much do they need to know so that they are prepared to meet the world? How much can they handle, and at what point does truth, when it is terrible, faith destroying, hope-destroying, unassimilable truth, become unsuitable for children, with their still undeveloped capacities to sustain its reception? (p. 210).

In consideration of these questions, the aim of this work is to perform an exploration into the "double text" (Knoepflmacher, 2005) of Tony Kushner and Maurice Sendak's picturebook, *Brundibar*—named one of *The New York Times* Book Review's Ten Best Illustrated Children's Books of 2003—within a discussion of navigating the difficult terrain of worlds of "trouble and woe and worse" in children's literature. In this article, I will provide a discussion of (1) *Brundibar*'s historical context; (2) a semiotic analysis of the story and its illustrations, including a discussion of Krása and Hoffmeister's operetta; (3) the development of the Hitlerian Brundibar, and Sendak's alternate conceptions for the character; and (4) the pedagogical implications for reading difficult texts with children.

A Tragic Context: Hans Krása's *Brundibár* and Terezín

In 1938, composer Hans Krása and librettist Adolf Hoffmeister wrote what is today Krása's most popular and most often performed work, *Brundibár* (Czech for "bumble bee"), a children's opera in two acts. The opera was originally written for a contest sponsored by the Czech Ministry of Education; however, when the Nazis annexed Czechoslovakia in 1939, the contest was cancelled and no winner was announced (Witthoefft, 1999; Kushner, 2003; Červinková, 2005). Given the tenuous political circumstances during the Nazi occupation, it was not until five years after his original writing of the children's opera that Krása had the opportunity to see *Brundibár* performed for the very first time under unforeseeably grim circumstances.

After the annexation, Hoffmeister emigrated to France, while Krása remained behind in Prague, having given up on the long and arduous process of obtaining a visa abroad. Hoffmeister later said of waiting in line at the visa office that, "Krása was here, but lost the nerve. He couldn't stand it, waiting on line for five to eight hours straight. He gave up" (as cited in Červinková, 2005, p. 132). The fate of Krása, who was Jewish, might have been different had he continued to wait on line with Hoffmeister. However, on August 10, 1942, he was sent to Terezín (Theresienstadt), a Nazi concentration camp located 40 miles north of Prague.

Despite Hoffmeister's emigration, Krása's internment, and the political uncertainty and unsafe atmosphere for Jews in Prague, *Brundibár* made its debut performance toward the end of 1942 at a Vinohrady Jewish Boys' Orphanage in the city. In place of Krása, Rudolf Freudenfeld, the son of the orphanage director, took charge of the opera's musical direction, with Rafael Schächter conducting and František Zelenka in charge of set design. Freudenfeld recounted how difficult it became to sustain the practices as the children and adults working on the opera were gradually sent to Terezín: "The first transports were ordered. Rafík (Schächter) left, the children left, Krása left, then more children. We couldn't keep it together. During this time we also learned to use every moment of relaxation productively, as we were prepared for the worst" (p. 145). The worst did come, and in July 1943, Freudenfeld and the rest of the children from the orphanage were deported to Terezín, where they were eventually reunited with Krása. In a single act that would eventually ensure *Brundibár*'s future as Krása's most famous and most performed work, Freudenfeld successfully smuggled the piano score from the children's opera into the camp.³

With the piano score in hand, Krása set to work rewriting *Brundibár* for the instruments at his disposal in Terezín (Červinková, 2005). The Nazis showcased Terezín as a "model" concentration camp and allowed prisoners to engage in cultural activities to show the world how "well" they treated inmates. From early on in his internment, Krása engaged himself in the cultural life of the camp and became director of music selections for the "Freizeitgestaltung", or free time activities that the Nazis allowed Terezín prisoners to partake in. On September 23, 1943, the debut performance of *Brundibár* took place in the Magdeburger Barracks at Terezín and proved a great success. Given the grim context of the performances, the audience soon read a deeper meaning into *Brundibár*; one of bullying and oppression, not dissimilar to their own experience being brutally bullied under Nazi domination (Karas, 1996). As a result of its success and resonance with camp audiences, *Brundibár* is officially documented as having been performed at Terezín a total of 55 times.

As questions surfaced about the horrific conditions under which prisoners lived and perished in Nazi concentration camps, the International Red Cross arranged an

---

³ Freudenfeld's smuggling of the score into Terezín provided inspiration for Kushner's *But the Giraffe!*, the playlet that opened Kushner and Sendak's stage production of *Brundibar* (Isherwood, 2006), which premiered at the Berkeley Repertory Theatre in 2005.

"investigative" visit to Terezín, which took place on June 23, 1944. In preparation for the Red Cross and in a cruel act of deception, Terezín was transformed into a "Potemkin village"[4] of sorts (Červinková, 2005, p. 170), which provided an arguably convincing façade to the gruesome reality of day-to-day life in the camp. To complete the deception of Terezín as a "model" camp, the Nazis attended to the aesthetic details of cleaning the streets, freshly painting the buildings, planting trees, erecting storefronts, finely clothing and feeding prisoners (and transporting "excess" prisoners to their deaths to diminish the appearance of overcrowding), as well as showcasing the cultural activities of the camp. *Brundibár* was performed for the Red Cross Commission as one of the cultural highlights to show the "fine life" that Jews lived in Terezín.

The children's opera was performed again for propaganda purposes during the filming of *Der Führer schenkt die Jüden eine Stadt* ("The Führer Gives the Jews a City"), to show the world how "well" the Nazis were treating the Jews. The Nazis wanted *Brundibár*'s success to be relived during the 1945 Red Cross visit, but as Červinková (2005) points out, "This was, however, no longer possible. Most of the children who had worked on *Brundibár* were no longer living. Freudenfeld, Zelenka, and Krása were no longer there" (p. 173). Hans Krása was transported to Auschwitz on October 16, 1944, where he perished like so many innocent others. It is through *Brundibár* that his music and spirit live on.[5]

Brundibar: A Semiotic Walk Through Kushner and Sendak's Picturebook

The Peritext

An important starting point for analyzing the semiotic structure of the text and illustrations in Kushner and Sendak's *Brundibar* is to begin by carefully examining the dust jacket and front and back covers (Sipe, 2008). On the glossy, dust jacket cover, we encounter the young brother-sister pair, Pepicek (dressed in tones of green and blue) and Aninku (in tones of red and yellow), for the first time. The two children run across a brightly colored, moonlit and flower-lined path, connected by the red milk pail they carry between them. They are clearly in a hurry to get somewhere, perhaps to their mother, or into the story, but the smiles on their faces show that the children are both hopeful and excited. However, we might wonder what two young children are doing running around at night, unattended by an adult. Some questions this cover might raise are: Why are the children in such a hurry? What is the bucket for? Where are their parents?

---

[4] The term "Potemkin village" comes from Grigory Potemkin, the prime minister to Catherine the Great of Russia. When Catherine the Great chose to take a cruise on the Danube, which was a very impoverished region of the empire, it is alleged that Potemkin had impressive fake villages and cheering peasants ready to greet her and act as a façade to the great poverty that existed there (Maxwell, 2005).

[5] As for the original Brundibár score, submitted to the children's opera contest in 1938, it is said to have remained in the Ministry of Education office until 1972 when it was discovered by the widow of Jaroslav Jindra, a former Czech attaché to Vienna. Jindra's widow donated the score to the Terezín Memorial (Červinková, 2005).

In removing the brightly colored dust jacket from the book, the reader is confronted with the ominous sepia cloth cover, blindstamped with the indelible, black ink signature of Brundibar. The dark brown cover can be said to evoke the Brownshirts of Hitler's *Sturmabteilung* (L. Sipe, personal communication, November 11, 2010), while the black stamp of Brundibar's signature harkens the SA's terrible maxim, "All opposition must be stamped into the ground" (Mitcham, 1996, p. 139). The dust jacket can also be viewed as a colorful, optimistic façade covering the grisly underlying context of *Brundibar*, similar to the Nazi deception and presentation of Terezín to the world as a model concentration camp.

As we open *Brundibar's* front cover, endpapers depict the outline of a young boy flying on the back of a raven. This same image appears in the nightmarish and allegorical "flight of the children" scene later in the book. On both the front and back endpapers, this outline appears as a translational symmetry pattern, colored in tones of light red and pink; colors that remind us of the living flesh and blood that were quashed under Nazi terror. Lest we forget *Brundibar* is a children's opera, these endpapers can also be viewed as "stage curtains framing the performance" (Sipe, 2008, p. 254). Let the show begin!

The establishing shot of *Brundibar* appears on the half-title page and gives the hurried Pepicek and Aninku a chance to introduce themselves to us. Pepicek, trying to catch up to his sister, holding on to his hat so it does not blow away: "I am Pepicek, very small." Aninku running ahead of her brother with milk pail in hand, taking a moment to graciously curtsey to her audience: "And I am Aninku, his sister, even smaller." Overhead, a black raven follows the children, despite their youth, like the shadow of death; the mythic status of ravens, carrion-eaters, has been attributed to their role as mediators between life and death (Lévi-Strauss, 1955). Moreover, the composition of the half-title page is unsettling, because of the white space that the children hover in. They are not grounded, and while we know they are running somewhere, it appears as though they could fall into the nothingness (Bang, 2000).

The title page shows a cutaway of the small house in the "yellow hills" that the children live in with their mother. Only today is not a happy day for the family, because mommy is very sick, her face sallow and hands green. The raven is present again, perched atop the house and perhaps waiting for the worst to befall the children's mother. Turning the page to the front matter, we see the mother calling for the children to, "Quick! Fetch the doctor!" The children come running to their mother across the dedication page with the Jewish doctor (indicated by the yellow star on his jacket), a "Sendakian look-alike" (Knoepflmacher, 2005, p. 172), in tow. These events all transpire before the official first page of the story, providing the context for the children's journey that Krása and Hoffmeister's opera implies, but does not portray. These "pre-story" events also remind us that there is no time to waste, neither in helping mommy, nor in getting the performance underway, because death is waiting on the turn of a page.

The Journey Begins

With their mother looking quite ill and a triumvirate of ravens flying over their house, the doctor urges the children to run to town and fetch the much needed milk for their mother. Wasting no time, the children reach hurriedly for the empty milk pail, whose red hue reminds us that milk is the crucial lifeblood and doctor-prescribed panacea for their ailing mother. This same milk pail becomes a barometer of Pepicek and Aninku's effort to save their mother; our hearts sink when it is empty, and our spirits rise when it is finally filled with money, then milk. In an unfortunate role reversal, the children are placed in the position of mother as the provider of milk and life, and as nourishers (Knoepflmacher, 2005). If the situation were not urgent enough, Pepicek and Aninku recall that their daddy died when they were babies and that they "don't remember him at all." These small children are at risk of becoming orphans, like the real-life children in the Vinohrady Jewish Boys Orphanage in Prague and the child survivors of the Holocaust, who lost their parents to the Nazi gas chambers and crematoria.

As the old doctor sends the children away, we might wonder why he did not fetch the milk himself. Given that he is Jewish, as indicated by the yellow Star of David on his overcoat, it can be conjectured that it is perhaps too dangerous for him to walk the town streets. It is also possible that the doctor believes it is more important that he stay behind to care for the children's mother. In Krása and Hoffmeister's *Brundibár*, the milkman scolds the children when they ask for milk, "Who needs a doctor's care? That's for the wealthy. I sell a better ware, fresh milk is healthy…But if you don't have a quarter, your poor kitten must lap water" (Krása and Hoffmeister, 1996, Track 4). We can't help but feel that the children have been placed in a terrible catch-22, which the milkman is quick to point out; instead of paying for a doctor, they should have just purchased milk. But how could they have known to purchase milk without calling for the doctor?

As the children near the town square in Kushner and Sendak's *Brundibar* after "a long trip, a hot trip", they encounter a number of colorful, but unhelpful adults, who tell them, "You want milk? Then go to the town square!" The children we see in the background, as Pepicek and Aninku move from the town outskirts to the town square, appear washed-out, lifeless, and neglected. Adults pass these children by and pay them no attention. We are also reminded that this picturebook takes place in Nazi-occupied Prague, as another man passes by with a yellow star embroidered on his overcoat. In this scene, Pepicek and Aninku arrive in the town where "everyone everyone everyone was there, buying buying busy buying" as if to remind them that they, as poor children, have no buying power themselves.

The Ice-Cream Seller

Once in the town square, the children encounter the terrifyingly clown-like and garishly-colored ice-cream seller, who offers his abundance of ice cream cones to children who can pay. However, we might wonder if he is just out to turn a profit or to bring children joy. He sings that his "ice cream's so cold it burns! Greedy folk who gobble hasty will turn blue and pucker-faced-y", and seems aloof to the crying children who have dropped their ice cream, lost it to a hungry raven, or simply can't afford to buy it. This ice-cream seller's song is darker than the one sung by Krása and Hoffmeister's ice-cream seller, who calls out to his customers, "Come and get your ice cream. It's so cold, it pleases all. Everyone loves ice cream, young and old and big and small" (1996, Track 4). In Sendak's illustration, Pepicek and Aninku are positioned in the lower left corner of the page, with their heads hung low and eyes closed as a blood-red gob of ice-cream blobs off of the ice-cream seller's foot and onto Pepicek's hat. In Sendak's positioning of the children, we can see they are "down in the dumps" (Bang, 2000, p. 56) as they realize that this adult will not help them.

The Baker

Next the children encounter an Oliver Hardy-esque baker, reminiscent of the three bakers in another Sendak tale in which milk is a crucial plot ingredient, *In the Night Kitchen* (1970). To fully illustrate the baker's excess juxtaposed against Pepicek and Aninku's dire need, Kushner describes how the baker with "his face like a sticky bun, raisin eyes and a round red knob of a nose, shook his jelly-jowls." Sendak's illustration corroborates this description as we see the small Pepicek and Aninku reaching for the fine breads and pastries cascading over the baker's arm, just out of their reach. The ravens are feasting again without the baker's notice, this time on the best part of his treats: the cherry on top. Pepicek and Aninku's red milk pail sits empty at the baker's feet to remind us that they still do not have milk for mommy and that time is running out.

The Milkman

As they move on from the baker, the children rejoice when they finally see the milkman, the savior whose help they have been seeking since their critical journey began. Pepicek and Aninku wave from behind a fence that separates them from the milkman's path. The Czech word *škola* (school) is scrawled on the fence, resembling the stage set as it appears in photos and video of the Terezín production of *Brundibár* (Červinková, 2005, p. 170), and can perhaps be viewed as Sendak's tribute to that ill-fated production. This reference to *škola*, might also cause us to consider the grim-circumstances preventing Pepicek and Aninku from attending school like the other children, much as the children in Terezín were deprived of their right to attend school and enjoy childhood like the children outside of Terezín's walls.

The milkman, covered in a kindle of kittens and a single raven indulging in his wares from Mléko's Dairy (*mléko* is Czech for "milk"), like the ice-cream seller and baker who came before him, does not seem to notice the animals feasting on his goods. Either these peddlers truly do not notice the animals, or they are less opposed to feeding animals than children. If the latter is the case, these men are no better than the soon to be encountered organ-grinder Brundibar, who shouts at the children later in the book when they turn themselves into bears to scare him: "They're worse than bears, they're children!" The valuing of animal life over human life was made grotesquely apparent by the Nazis, particularly at Buchenwald, where a small zoo was installed just feet from the camp fence for the pleasure of SS officers (Siebeck, 2009) and for the malnourished prisoners to see the animals being fed daily as they continued to go hungry.

Meanwhile, the milkman sings a ditty that promises fresh milk for "kiddies", "mudders" and "cats." What he does not include in his song is how payment is a prerequisite for the requisite milk. He repeats the word "milk" so many times that there is no doubt that he should be the adult to help the children acquire milk for their mother:

> Milk, oh! Milk, oh! Farm-fresh milk, oh!
> Milk for kiddies, milk for mudders,
> Milk for cats, from Bessie's udders!
> Fresh cold milk, oh, milk, oh, milk, oh,
> Butter too, and cheese.

In the milkman montage, Sendak evokes his earlier work, *We Are All in the Dumps with Jack and Guy*. The kittens in the milkman's cart are reminiscent of the kidnapped kittens on their way to St. Paul's Bakery and Orphanage, perhaps foreshadowing Pepicek and Aninku's fate as orphans if they do not succeed in bringing home milk to their mother. We also see two pale children in rags resembling "dumps children", living in a Jewish cemetery. It is certain if these sickly children do not find food, clothing, and shelter soon, the cemetery will become their permanent home.

Passing by these ghostly children, Pepicek and Aninku run to the milkman with the empty milk pail in their outstretched arms, pleading, "Please, we need milk for mommy who is sick." The milkman scolds the children, "First you give me money, then I'll give you milk." As he reprimands the children, the kittens' mother appears from behind and steals the milkman's milk, butter, cheese, and cart with her kittens in it, much like the moon/cat that intervenes in *We Are All in the Dumps with Jack and Guy*. Hardly noticing that his wares are being snatched by an imposing mother cat, the milkman shoos Pepicek and Aninku away as if *they* were animals: "No money? No milk! Now skedaddle!" Like the other adults the children have encountered, the milkman is in no mood to help two small children in need.

The Organ-Grinder Brundibar

The organ-grinder, Brundibar, is a terrible sight to behold in his ragged Napoleonic hat and tattered brown frock, studded with military regalia. His "moustache that threatens to become rat's whiskers" and "staring eyes of psychopathic blue" (Kushner, 2003, p. 210) remind us of Hitler's infamous toothbrush moustache and his obsession with the blond-haired, blue-eyed "Aryan" race. He is the unfortunate antithesis of the elderly and freezing Müllerian *Leiermann* (German for "organ-grinder"), made famous in Franz Schubert's (1828) *Winterreise* song cycle, who stands in the cold of winter grinding his organ with an empty coin plate and no audience to listen to his music. Brundibar the organ-grinder is far more captivating and potent. Singing an awful song, Brundibar cranks his hurdy-gurdy, decorated with a black raven and iron cross. His monkey, with the distinct face of Hitler's propaganda minister, Joseph Goebbels (L. Sipe, personal communication, November 11, 2010) wears a *Pickelhaube* in the Prussian style and collects coins from Brundibar's captive audience. "Bravo, Brundibar!" they shout. We are left wondering how any adults could appreciate and throw their money at this ghastly duo. However, their bizarre performance appears to speak to people of all ages, as we see two pale-colored, pencil-sketched Jewish children dancing to his song in the background. These children's near colorlessness is juxtaposed with Brundibar and his monkey's vibrant water-colored glory. We are reminded yet again that time is running out for Pepicek and Aninku to save their mother and themselves.

Inspired by Brundibar's act, the children attempt to sing for money to buy milk for their mommy. However, the other children and adults are too entranced by Brundibar's performance to pay any attention to Pepicek and Aninku's song. The children become so angry at the lack of attention that they turn themselves into bears in an effort to scare Brundibar away. In return for the prank and for frightening his audience, Brundibar sings them a horrible song: "Little children, how I hate 'em/ How I wish the bedbugs ate 'em/ When they're rude and answer back/ Stuff 'em in a burlap sack!/ Nasty little children, quiet/ Don't be loud, don't even try it/ You'll find out what troubles are/ If you bother Brundibar!" (Kushner and Sendak, 2003). Kushner's libretto, with its direct references to bedbugs eating children and children being stuffed into burlap sacks as punishment for their disobedience, is in some ways more grotesque than Hoffmeister's version of Brundibár's song, yet milder than the preliminary lyrics that Kushner and Sendak had considered in an earlier conceptualization of the picturebook. These preliminary lyrics will be discussed subsequently.

It is apparent from Hoffmeister's libretto that the bully Brundibár is a Hitlerian figure, who cannot be bothered with child dissenters. His song commands the obedience and respect of those under his dictatorship: "Doggone children, what a bother!/ If I only were their father/ I would teach proper manners,/ Courtesy, respect and honour./ And you kids, don't make a riot./ Where I rule you must be quiet./ Here's my empire. I'm the czar,/ Organ-grinder Brundibár" (Krása and Hoffmeister, 1996, Track 8). Much as Hitler purged those he deemed "undesirable" and in opposition to him, Brundibár threatens a world of hurt and pain to those who do not sing his foul song. He continues: "When I play and turn this handle./ Sing with me, don't make a scandal!/ Don't you like my music making?/ Out of here or you'll be aching!/ Of this show I am the star,/ I, organ-grinder, Brundibár!" (Krása and Hoffmeister, 1996, Track 8). The song of Krása and Hoffmeister's Brundibár frames the character as a dictator, which is indicated by his reference to himself as a czar ruling his empire. Kushner and Sendak's Brundibar, on the other hand, comes across as a spoiled and vindictive older child, who is angry that "little children" have attempted to steal his spotlight.

Kushner and Sendak struggled with how to represent Brundibar; agonizing over how closely the character should resemble Hitler. Of Sendak's initial sketches of Brundibar as Hitler (see Figs. 1, 2), Kushner (2003) wrote:

> It was too horrible, and it raised all the old questions. When you are reading this book to a child, are you meant to stop and explain to the kid who this scary-looking man was, or what he'd done? I felt the choice we'd made was unfair to parents, and inappropriate to the tale, to the impulse to present an

> This illustration is available in the journal Children's Literature in Education, (2012) volume 43, issue 01, pages 27–47. DOI: 10.1007/s10583-011-9158-8. Due to Maurice Sendak's passing it was unfortunately not possible to arrange the permission in a timely manner for the figure to be included in this book.

Fig. 1 Preliminary drawing for *Brundibar*. Pencil and colored pencil. © 2001 by Maurice Sendak, all rights reserved

> This illustration is available in the journal Children's Literature in Education, (2012) volume 43, issue 01, pages 27–47. DOI: 10.1007/s10583-011-9158-8. Due to Maurice Sendak's passing it was unfortunately not possible to arrange the permission in a timely manner for the figure to be included in this book.

Fig. 2 Preliminary drawing for *Brundibar*. Pencil on tracing paper. © 2002 by Maurice Sendak, all rights reserved

allegory…Maurice went back to work, and made the decision to turn Brundibar back into a boy (p. 210).

In addition to the horrible figure that a true image of Hitler would have presented in the picturebook, Kushner's lyrics for Brundibar's song (see Table 1; Fig. 1) were far more terrifying than the lyrics he and Sendak chose for final publication. As can be seen in Sendak's preliminary drawing of this scene (see Fig. 1), Brundibar cranks

Table 1 A comparison of Brundibar's songs to scare the children away, from the original libretto and Kushner and Sendak's preliminary and final texts

Hoffmeister's Libretto	Kushner and Sendak's Preliminary Text	Kushner and Sendak's Final Text
Doggone children, what a bother! If I only were their father I would teach proper manners, Courtesy, respect and honour. And you kids, don't make a riot. Where I rule you must be quiet. Here's my empire. I'm the czar, Organ-grinder Brundibár. When I play and turn this handle. Sing with me, don't make a scandal! Don't you like my music making? Out of here or you'll be aching! Of this show I am the star, I, organ-grinder, Brundibár! (Krása & Hoffmeister, 1996, Track 8)	Little children, how I hate 'em How I wish the bedbugs ate 'em How their parents overrate 'em If they're rude exterminate 'em	Little children, how I hate 'em How I wish the bedbugs ate 'em When they're rude and answer back Stuff 'em in a burlap sack! Nasty little children, quiet Don't be loud, don't even try it You'll find out what troubles are If you bother Brundibar! (Kushner & Sendak, 2003)

his hurdy-gurdy, shakes an angry fist at the children and sings: "Little children, how I hate 'em/ How I wish the bedbugs ate 'em/ How their parents overrate 'em/ If they're rude exterminate 'em." It is possible that Kushner and Sendak decided that this particular lyric crossed a line, considering the countless children—including those from the Terezín production of *Brundibár*—who were exterminated at Auschwitz and other Nazi concentration camps. The author and illustrator envisioned *Brundibar* as a book that "honors the martyred dead" (Kushner, 2003, p. 210), and such an overtly horrible libretto might have detracted from their original intent for the book. Instead, their Brundibar sings a still terrible song in the final published version of the picturebook (see Table 1), but without the overt reference to extermination.

In Kushner and Sendak's version, Brundibar's song becomes so vitriolic that "his eyes turned pink" and "his face turned purple", scaring the small and helpless Pepicek and Aninku, who are simply trying to buy milk for their mother. Sendak draws Brundibar's huge and awful face rising up from behind the fence (on which we can see Sendak's tribute to Hans Krása scrawled) against a rage red sky. In an act of solidarity with Brundibar, the adults, the other children, and even the animals jeer at Pepicek and Aninku, whose pencil-sketched color appears to be fading against the watercolored vibrancy of the others. It is clear that the children are growing weaker at the expense of Brundibar and his followers growing more powerful. In one of his preliminary drawings for this scene (see Fig. 2), Sendak's Brundibar appears again as an explicitly Hitlerian figure with a signature toothbrush moustache and peaked military cap. This Brundibar waves a huge fist that threatens to crush the children. Additionally, the fence in this preliminary drawing bears the word *Jude* (German for "Jew")—as it appeared written on the yellow badges that Jewish men, women and children were forced to wear in public under Nazi rule— rather than Hans Krása's name. Pepicek and Aninku would not have stood a chance in the face of such a ghastly foe.

It is at this point in Sendak and Kushner's picturebook that the once vibrant hues of its illustrations grow more tinted to create a darker mood. Kushner (2003) writes:

> The first images, those in the "real" part of the book, are simple, brightly colored...After the kids hide in the alley and meet their animal rescuers, after our fantasy or their dream has begun to take over, Maurice's drawings assume a greater degree of elaboration, historical specificity, of gritty reality. (p. 214)

Knoepflmacher (2005) recounts Sendak's appearance in November 2003 with Kushner at a performance of their stage-version of *Brundibar* at New York's 92nd Street "Y". Sendak said of Pepicek and Aninku, "In my mind they died." However, according to Knoepflmacher, Sendak insisted that the children's fantasy of overcoming the Hitlerian bully should be viewed as uplifting, much in the same way as we view Hansel and Gretel killing and "The fantasy of killing the witch—for the witch-mother can't get away with these things" (pp. 172–173).

Pepicek and Aninku in the Dumps

After Brundibar's tirade, the dejected children sit alone in a dark alleyway among abandoned and empty shoes, coats, hats, and a baby carriage. Knoepflmacher (2005) points out that these abandoned articles further support Sendak's argument that the children died along with the others who perished in the Holocaust. Their milk pail is kicked over, perhaps alluding to "kicking the bucket," another substantiation of the children's death. Like the dumps children, Pepicek and Aninku tragically sit in empty milk boxes, covered in newspapers that report (translated from the Czech): "Kafka will be next president", "Kafka on the castle", "Opera does not have the money", and the German text of the invitation to the performance of *Brundibár* at Terezín, which appears in ticket format on the last page of the picturebook. As Pepicek and Aninku sink further into the newspapers and more empty shoes pile up around them, a sparrow, cat, and dog come to their rescue, unlike the countless adults who have ignored the children, jeered at them, or refused to help them. The animals encourage Pepicek and Aninku to request the help of others. In a world of unhelpful adults, Pepicek and Aninku's only choice is to turn to other children.

Children Uniting Against the Bully

This morbid alleyway scene blends into the scene of school kids crossing bridges that span over an "Arbeit macht frei" banner, the infamous motto of Auschwitz, which translates into "Work sets you free". This bridge crossing evokes the scene in *Dear Mili* when Mili is lost in the forest and dead victims of the Holocaust can be seen in the distance, crossing a bridge before a silhouette of Auschwitz. Other banners in this scene of children (translated from the Czech) read: "Victory! Terezín Ghetto" and "children's playground." Again, we see the raven lurking in the lower right corner. As we soon learn, these school kids "don't mind skipping school" because they believe in "Milk for mommy!" and that "Bullies must be defied!" Pepicek and Aninku enlist the help of these 300 school children. To show that they have not yet given up hope, Aninku holds the red milk pail in her hand once more. This signifies the beginning of the children's fantasy of overcoming the bully.

All 302 children march to the town square where Brundibar is performing, and demand that they have a chance to sing for money. Brundibar refuses, yelling: "Oho you cannot! That's my racket!" However, this time, the adults tell Brundibar to "Shush!" because they want to hear the children sing a lullaby. The lullaby they sing is haunting, indeed, about a baby blackbird who grows up too quickly, leaving the cradle cold and the mother alone by herself to grow old. This song leads into the terrifying double-page spread of helpless mothers pleading and sobbing into their arms as their children fly away on the backs of blackbirds. Perhaps these mothers weep because they could not save their children from the horror of a cruel and untimely death.

Thankfully, the adults love the children's song and hurl their money into the "marvelous wonderful children's soon-to-be-milkbucket." The dream of milk for mommy seems closer than ever, but Brundibar and his monkey steal the red pail filled with money and run away. The cat, dog, sparrow, 302 children, 1,000 grown-ups, and cop follow in pursuit. The three ravens we saw hovering over Pepicek and Aninku's house at the beginning of the story are now chasing Brundibar, perhaps foreshadowing his impending death. The dog, looking rabid, clamps down hard with his razor-sharp teeth on Brundibar's buttock, while the cat, sparrow, and ravens viciously peck and claw at him. Brundibar has met his end. Or has he?

Home Again

While we never see the grisly end we can only assume Brundibar meets, we must fill in this indeterminacy with our imagination (Iser, 1978). Sipe and Brightman (2009) suggest that when reading texts with children that include indeterminacies inherent in the page breaks, teachers should "position children as active co-authors of the story rather than passive recipients of unconnected plot elements or episodes" (p. 78). Kushner and Sendak leave it up to us, the readers, to determine Brundibar's fate.

After what we might interpret to be the children's triumph over Brundibar, Pepicek and Aninku return home with a full pail of fresh milk for their mother. Unlike the concluding scene in *Dear Mili*, in which Mili comes home to her corpse-like mother, Pepicek and Aninku's mother appears well, giving her two small children hugs and kisses. While the individual reader might determine otherwise, let us not forget that Kushner and Sendak believe that Pepicek and Aninku died, and that they envision the second portion of the story as the children's *post mortem* fantasy of defeating Brundibar. Therefore, it might be possible to interpret *Dear Mili* and *Brundibar* as having very similar fatal and unhappy endings. To further support the possibility that the children and their mother have passed on, we see a crucifix hanging from the wall, either denoting that the family is Christian, or that they have died as martyrs because of the world's sins against them. The doctor cheerfully wishes the family, "Mazel Tov!" and dances out of the house. His work is done.

The children who united themselves with Pepicek and Aninku appear once more to proclaim: "The wicked never win! We have our victory yet! Tyrants come along, but you just wait and see! They topple one-two-three! Our friends make us strong! And thus we end our song!" The ultimate crushing irony is that "the wicked" often do "win" (L. Sipe, personal communication, February 15, 2011). The children's proclamation against tyrants echoes Emil Saudek's altering of the last few lines of the Hoffmeister's libretto for *Brundibár*, which initially read: "He who so loves his mother and father and his native land is our friend and can play with us." Saudek changed the text to read, "He who loves justice and can defend it and who is not afraid, is our friend and can play with us" (Karas, 1996). Saudek's version raises some important existential questions: What does it mean to love your family in a cruel and unjust world? What does it mean to love your native land when it no longer loves you? Let us not forget that many of the children who performed *Brundibár* were orphans in both the familial and national sense, having been separated from their loved ones and living in a land that no longer saw them as valuable and legitimate members of society. It is perhaps the reality of these injustices that caused Kushner and Sendak to not end *Brundibar* just yet.

Kushner's Chilling Coda

The hopeful closing words of the victorious children might signal the end of this picturebook in a perfect world. However, Kushner chose to let Brundibar have the last words. In an interview with Terry Gross (2006), Sendak stated that Kushner added the chilling coda at the end of the book, which can again be sung to the melody of Brundibár's song in Krása's operetta: "They believe they've won the fight, / They believe I'm gone—not quite. / Nothing ever works out neatly— / Bullies don't give up completely. / One departs, the next appears, / And we shall meet again, my dears! / Though I go, I won't go far…/ I'll be back. Love,/ Brundibar."

Brundibar's ominous last words lead us to wonder if the children's proclamation that, "The wicked never win!" is perhaps an overly optimistic and idealistic statement. Brundibar's avowed return signifies that this is not a "Never Again" narrative (Sokoloff, 2005, p. 177), because injustice continues to plague children and families across the world today. Both history and the present day conflicts around the world have shown us that Brundibar as a tyrannical construct is still alive and well, causing us to wonder if he ever left. Furthermore, by not identifying Brundibar's character so closely with Hitler, it could be argued that Kushner and Sendak emphasize the unfortunate perpetuation of evil within and beyond the context of the Holocaust.

Pedagogical Implications for "Trouble and Woe and Worse" in Children's Literature

Classroom reading of children's literature with troubling double texts such as *Brundibar* can be problematic for teachers. Not only might the subject matter of the historical context prove difficult for teachers to reconcile with and teach, but students may find it problematic as well. Robertson (1997) explores the reaction of pre-service teachers to another difficult text, *Nightjohn* by Gary Paulsen (1993), within a psychoanalytical framework. She asserts, "Language arts teachers face a formidable task when they attempt to teach children about the sanctity of life through literary encounters with worlds of pain" (p. 457). Robertson evokes Simon and Armitage Simon's (1995) notion of the "shadow text" (as cited in Robertson, p. 462) that children (and adults) create to protect themselves from the disturbing ideas and images raised in risky texts, and defines the shadow text as "a story the ego tells itself in an attempt to guide its own confusions or dismay in the face of difficult knowledge" (p. 462).

It is possible that reading a story like *Brundibar*, given its full historical context, will cause children and teachers to create shadow texts to protect themselves from the difficult realities the Holocaust presents. While Kushner and Sendak, as stated earlier, did not want to burden parents with having to explain to their children who Hitler was and what he did, Sokoloff (2005) expresses concern that texts which aim to teach children about the Holocaust omit discussions of the political factors that would enable children to speak out against such atrocities should they emerge again. Furthermore, Kokkola (2003) points out that reading the Holocaust into works of fiction is only possible "when readers are already familiar with the events of the Holocaust" and are aware that "the Holocaust refers to an actual historical event" (p. 68). Some scholars also fear that representations of the Holocaust trivialize its memory. Ellsworth (2005) cautions, "the proliferation of efforts to represent the unrepresentable [Holocaust] and to understand that which exceeds all frames of cognition threatens to trivialize" (p. 101).

The double text of Kushner and Sendak's *Brundibar*, like the two versions of Krása and Hoffmeister's operetta, the original written for the Czech Ministry of Education and the other in Terezín (Červinková, 2005), offers two versions of the story: one about bullying and another about bullying in the midst of the Holocaust's horrors. Another issue that the double text raises, considering that it is in picturebook format is: When is it appropriate to introduce children to the Holocaust? Bosmajian (2009) fears that if the project of "tropes of trauma" were to traumatize young readers, the author and narrative of such works would become perpetrators responsible for "inflicting trauma transgressively" (p. 296). She cautions writers and critics who propose that young readers should face what 'the Holocaust was really about,' to consider the implications of such trauma. Bosmajian adds that teaching what 'the Holocaust was really about' is, in itself, an impossible task. The controversy around attempts to portray the Holocaust is evidence that "it is still taboo-laden to speak of creative art from within the Holocaust" (Rovit, 2000).

As troubling as the Holocaust is, it is also possible that children, particularly at the middle and upper grade levels, will be more engaged by the concerns, issues, and dilemmas portrayed in texts that bother and disturb them (Galda and Beach, 2001). However, this does not solve the dilemma of when and how to introduce the Holocaust to young children. Sendak and Kushner's *Brundibar* gives teachers and parents the option of how to approach the text, but it can be argued that this option allows adults an "easy out" in choosing whether or not to expose children to the cruel fate met by *Brundibár*'s composer and most of its cast. Bosmajian (2002) asserts, "Desire and unresolved grief constitute the main subtextual tensions in narratives for the young about Nazism; desire for normal life and a necessarily unresolved grief for those who perished characterize Holocaust narratives" (p. xv). These subtextual tensions are present in *Brundibar*: Pepicek and Aninku desire a normal life, in which their mother is healthy and strong; but, the children's death and enactment of a fantasy trope reminds us of how Brundibar and the Holocaust prevent the children from achieving their desire.

While it is important to protect young children from trauma, Sendak reminds us that children, as naive as we hope and want them to be in a world of "trouble and woe and worse", are more acutely aware than we think. In the preface to *I Dream of Peace* (Grant and UNICEF, 1994), a collection of artwork and writings from children of the former Yugoslavia, he writes:

> The children know. They have always known. But we choose to think otherwise; it hurts to know the children know. The children see. If we obfuscate, they will not see. Thus we conspire to keep them from knowing and seeing. And if we *insist*, then the children, to please us, will make believe they do not know, they do not see. Children make that sacrifice for our sake—to keep us pacified. They are remarkably patient, loving, and all-forgiving. It is a sad comedy: the children knowing and pretending they don't know to protect us from knowing they know. (p. 5)

Conclusion

In conclusion, Tony Kushner and Maurice Sendak's *Brundibar* presents a difficult text with a difficult history. However, it is an important text with implications not only for teaching the Holocaust, but for exploring the countless examples of bullying prevalent in the world today. While the appropriateness of discussing the Holocaust with young children, and to what extent, is arguable, a child's reading of *Brundibar* might cause them to transact with the text in ways that bring their "unique reservoir of public and private significances, the residue of past experience with language and texts in life situations" (Rosenblatt, 1986). Children may very well read their own experiences with injustice into the text as a way of declaring solidarity with Pepicek and Aninku. However, it is not my goal here to speculate about children's responses to *Brundibar*, as I would prefer to invite children to respond to the text in a future study.

Acknowledgments In addition to Dr. Sipe's teaching and mentoring, I am also indebted to the scholarship of Dr. Blanka Červinková (1942–2002) for the in-depth research and interviews she conducted to create one of the few comprehensive biographies of Hans Krása. Without her scholarship, I might not have been able to adequately round out *Brundibár's* historical context within this work. I would also like to thank Patrick Rodgers, Traveling Exhibitions Coordinator at the Rosenbach Museum in Philadelphia, for sharing Maurice Sendak's preliminary and final drawings for *Brundibar* with me during my visit to the Rosenbach to complete my research for this article. Finally, I would like to thank my good friends and colleagues, Rachel Skrlac-Lo and Todd Bates, and my husband, Jonathan Larsen, for all of their encouragement and support throughout the many stages of this journey.

Children's Literature References

Grimm, Wilhelm, & Sendak, Maurice. (1988). *Dear Mili*. New York: Michael Di Capua.
Kushner, Tony, & Sendak, Maurice. (2003). *Brundibar*. New York: Michael Di Capua.
Paulsen, Gary. (1993). *Nightjohn*. New York: Bantam Doubleday Dell.
Sendak, Maurice. (1963). *Where the Wild Things Are*. New York: Harper Collins.
Sendak, Maurice. (1970). *In the Night Kitchen*. New York: Harper Collins.
Sendak, Maurice. (1981). *Outside over There*. New York: Harper Collins.
Sendak, Maurice. (1990). *We are All in the Dumps with Jack and Guy*. New York: Michael Di Capua.
Sendak, Maurice. (2011). *Bumble-Ardy*. New York: Michael Di Capua.

References

Bang, Molly. (2000). *Picture This: How Pictures Work*. San Francisco, CA: Chronicle Books.
Bangs, Lance (Director), & Jonze, Spike. (Director). (2010). *Tell Them Anything You Want: A Portrait of Maurice Sendak* [Motion picture]. United States: Oscilloscope Laboratories.
Bosmajian, Hamida. (2002). *Sparing the Child: Grief and the Unspeakable in Youth Literature About Nazism and the Holocaust*. New York: Routledge.
Bosmajian, Hamida. (2009). The Tropes of Trauma. *Children's Literature, 37*, 293–299.
Červinková, Blanka. (2005). *Hans Krása: Leben und Werk* (H. Smolíková, Trans. into German. Trans. into English, mine.). Saarbrücken: Pfau-Verlag.
Ellsworth, Elizabeth. (2005). *Places of Learning: Media, Architecture, Pedagogy*. New York: Routledge.
Fisher, James. (2008). *Understanding Tony Kushner* Columbia, SC: University of South Carolina Press.
Galda, Lee, & Beach, Richard. (2001). Response to Literature as a Cultural Activity. *Reading Research Quarterly, 36*(1), 64–73.
Grant, James P., & UNICEF. (1994). *I Dream of Peace: Images of War by Children of Former Yugoslavia*. New York: HarperCollins.
Gross, Terry. (Writer). (2006, May 5). *Sendak on Adapting 'Brundibar' for Theater* [Talk Radio Program]. Accessed November 28, 2010, from http://www.npr.org/templates/story/story.php?storyId=5386235.
Gross, Terry. (Writer). (2011, September 20). *This Pig Wants to Party: Maurice Sendak's Latest* [Talk Radio Program]. Accessed October 17, 2011, from http://www.npr.org/2011/09/20/140435330/this-pig-wants-to-party-maurice-sendaks-latest.
Inskeep, Steve. (Writer). (2006, September 26). *Why Maurice Sendak Puts Kids in Danger*. [Radio News Program]. Accessed December 8, 2010, from http://www.npr.org/templates/transcript/transcript.php?storyId=6139979.
Iser, Wolfgang. (1978). *The Act of Reading*. Baltimore: Johns Hopkins University Press.
Isherwood, Charles. (2006, May 9). Tony Kushner and Maurice Sendak Adapt 'Brundibar,' a Czech Children's Opera. *The New York Times*. Accessed December 1, 2010, from http://theater.nytimes.com/2006/05/09/theater/reviews/09brun.html?scp=1&sq=brundibar&st=cse.
Karas, Joža. (1996). Untitled Album Introduction. In *Hans Krása: Brundibár A Children's Opera in Two Acts, Hebrew and Yiddish Folk Songs* [CD]. (M. Javora & J. Karas, Trans.). New York: Arabesque Recordings.
Knoepflmacher, U.C. (2005). The Hansel and Gretel Syndrome: Survivorship Fantasies and Parental Discretion. *Children's Literature, 33*, 171–184.
Kokkola, Lydia. (2003). *Representing the Holocaust in Children's Literature*. New York: Routledge.
Krása, Hans, & Hoffmeister, Adolf. (1996). *Hans Krása: Brundibár A Children's Opera in Two Acts, Hebrew and Yiddish Folk Songs* [CD]. (M. Javora & J. Karas, Trans.). New York: Arabesque Recordings.
Kushner, Tony. (1992). *A Bright Room Called Day*. New York: Broadway Play Publishing.
Kushner, Tony. (1995). *Angels in America*. New York: Theater Communications Group.
Kushner, Tony. (2003). *The Art of Maurice Sendak: 1980 to the Present*. New York: Harry N. Abrams.
Kushner, Tony. (2006). Music with a Point. In *NewVicBill: Brundibar* (pp. 12–13). New York: The New Victory Theater on the New 42nd Street.
Lanes, Selma G. (1980). *The Art of Maurice Sendak*. New York: Abrams.

 Springer

Lévi-Strauss, Claude. (1955). The Structural Study of Myth. *The Journal of American Folklore, 682*(70), 428–444.
Maxwell, Joseph A. (2005). *Qualitative Research Design: An Interactive Approach* (2nd ed.). Thousand Oaks, CA: Sage Publications.
Mitcham, Samuel W. (1996). *Why Hitler? The Genesis of the Nazi Reich*. Santa Barabara, CA: Praeger.
Moyers, Bill. (Writer). (2004, March 12). *NOW with Bill Moyers* [Television broadcast]. New York: Public Broadcasting Service. Accessed December 3, 2010, from http://www.pbs.org/now/arts/sendak.html.
Pape, Walter. (1992). Happy Endings in a World of Misery: A Literary Convention Between Social Constraints and Utopia in Children's and Adult Literature. *Poetics Today, 13*(1), 179–196.
Robertson, Judith P. (1997). Teaching About Worlds of Hurt Through Encounters with Literature: Reflection on Pedagogy. *Language Arts, 74*(6), 457–466.
Rosenblatt, Louise M. (1986). The Aesthetic Transaction. *Journal of Aesthetic Education, 20*(4), 122–128.
Rovit, Rebecca. (2000). The "Brundibár" Project Memorializing Theresienstadt Children's Opera. *PAJ: A Journal of Performance and Art, 22*(2), 111–122.
Schubert, Franz. (1828). *Winterreise*, D. 911 (Op. 89). Vienna: Tobias Haslinger.
Sendak, Maurice. (1989). *Caldecott & Co.: Notes on Books and Pictures*. New York: Farrar, Straus & Giroux.
Shirk, Martha. (1989, December 4). Gloomy Relatives Inspired 'Wild Things' Author. *St. Louis Post-Dispatch*, p. 1D.
Siebeck, Cornelia. (2009). Humanize the Discourse! Non-Academic Reflections of a Memory Researcher. In C. Misselwitz & C. Siebeck (Eds.), *Dissonant Memories, Fragmented Present: Exchanging Young Discourses Between Israel and Germany* (pp. 75–84). Piscataway, NJ: Transaction Publishers.
Simon, Roger I., & Armitage Simon, W. (1995). Teaching Risky Stories: Remembering Mass Destruction Through Children's Literature. *English Quarterly, 28*(1), 27–31.
Sipe, Lawrence. (1996). The Private and Public Worlds of *We Are All in the Dumps with Jack and Guy*. *Children's Literature in Education, 27*(2), 87–108.
Sipe, Lawrence. (2008). *Storytime: Young Children's Literary Understanding in the Classroom*. New York: Teachers College Press.
Sipe, Lawrence R., & Brightman, Anne E. (2009). Young Children's Interpretations of Page Breaks in Contemporary Picturebooks. *Journal of Literacy Research, 41*, 68–103.
Sokoloff, Naomi. (2005). The Holocaust and Literature for Children. *Prooftexts, 25*, 174–194.
Witthoefft, Cornelis. (1999). Hans Krása. In *Komponisten in Theresienstadt* (pp. 32–42). Hamburg: Hans Krása Initiative (Translation mine).

Children's Literature in Education (2012) 43:48–50
DOI 10.1007/s10583-011-9150-3

COMMEMORATIVE ISSUE FOR DR. LAWRENCE SIPE

A Blissful Education

David Low

Published online: 15 February 2012
© Springer Science+Business Media, LLC 2012

Abstract A personal reflection from a student of Dr. Sipe showcases the power and humanity of his conversational prowess. In this reflection, a developing discussion with Dr. Sipe around Cynthia Rylant's *Missing May* (1992) is connected to Roland Barthes's concept of jouissance.

Keywords Lawrence Sipe · Jouissance · Roland Barthes · Missing May · Cynthia Rylant · Healing

A Blissful Education

Several months into our relationship—one I'd define by the bounded dyads of professor/student, mentor/mentee, and friend/friend—Dr. Lawrence Sipe introduced me to the word jouissance. The term, as employed by Roland Barthes, refers to the bliss experienced by a reader when he or she becomes immersed in a jarring text that "open[s] up new vistas of experience" (Sipe, 2008, p. 70). As Dr. Sipe explained it to me—and as I simplify here—jouissance is catharsis that emerges from becoming lost, and found, in the experience of difficult reading.

David Low is a PhD student at The University of Pennsylvania's Graduate School of Education. He has a particular focus on adolescent literacies, and the ways that multimodal reading and composing—primarily via the medium of comics and various sites of online media production—enable youths' meaning making and storytelling practices. Before attending Penn, David earned degrees from The University of Arizona and New York University, taught 10th and 11th grade English Language Arts in Tucson, and self-published a collection of single-panel cartoons.

D. Low (✉)
Reading/Writing/Literacy, Graduate School of Education, University of Pennsylvania, 3700 Walnut Street, Philadelphia, PA 19104, USA
e-mail: davidlow@gse.upenn.edu

I can no longer separate jouissance from my overriding memories of Dr. Sipe. As a scholar, as an educator, as a supremely beautiful human being, he experienced profound bliss in whichever direction he turned his attention. Dr. Sipe found his bliss in books, in reading and in writing them, in looking beyond words and pictures on the page to construct a text's gestalt. Dr. Sipe found his bliss in teaching, serving as the able conductor of a locomotive barreling toward new horizons of wonder and understanding. Dr. Sipe found his bliss in exploring and sharing in the art and ideas of others, and he found immeasurable bliss in laughing loudly with his friends, colleagues, and students. This is how I remember Dr. Sipe the most clearly.

On many afternoons I found myself cruising past his office door and, noticing it ajar, poked my head in for a quick hello. These salutes never went quite the way I planned: they were *never* quick. Dr. Sipe, with a friendly wave of the hand, swept me in, and invited me to take a load off. Before I knew it, we'd talked for an hour, swapping stories or discussing cooking, history, art, literature, children, academics. I can verily attest that in these conversations I experienced something akin to jouissance, so enrapturing and discombobulating were our chats.

A memory that stands out as resonantly blissful, in that pleasantly dislocative sense, involves a discussion Dr. Sipe and I had in 2010 around Cynthia Rylant's short Newbery Medal-winning novel *Missing May* (1992). In actuality, I'm not sure the word "discussion" even begins to cover it. This was more like a session in collaborative gumbo preparation, with Dr. Sipe and me strategically arranged around a burbling cauldron, throwing in whatever ingredients we had, in an effort to make something nutritious, bizarre, and spicy. Rylant's novel provided us with an excellent roux from which to work.

Before I continue, I must first acknowledge that my memories of this 'culinary' bull session have likely been altered greatly in the wake of Dr. Sipe's death. *Missing May*, I should mention, deals unflinchingly with death, sadness, and moving on. Following the news of Dr. Sipe's passing last spring, the book began to take on a new, embodied dimension for me, as I struggled, like several of Rylant's characters, to make some sense of how my academic life would function without one of its guiding forces. I found, again and again, my mind returning to our discussion of *Missing May*.

The character of seventh grader Cletus Underwood ("flat-out lunatic," "full of wonders") became the focus of our dialogue, due perhaps to his essential strangeness and wisdom. He serves as the novel's spiritual guide, lighting the paths of Summer and Ob (the bereaved, after May's death) to liberation and epiphany from beneath the shadow of loss. Gradually, our conversation unfolded outward to include Marcel Duchamp, Phil Ochs, and Maharishi Mahesh Yogi. Together, Dr. Sipe and I concocted, turn-by-turn, a tasty (if difficult to digest) gumbo of the sundry ingredients we brought into our understandings and extrapolations of Rylant's text. We discussed Cletus's propensity for re-appropriating spoons, potato chip bags, and Brylcreen advertisements—"anything with a story to it" (Rylant, 1992, p. 18)—in a way that riffed on Marcel Duchamp's readymades. We mused that the West Virginian troubadour Phil Ochs's song, "When I'm Gone" (1966), seemed superbly tailored to Rylant's themes of loss and re-actualization, and how splendid a connection, as the book itself takes place in West Virginia. I am including several lines of Ochs's song, in an effort to convey some of the tenor of our conversation, and also the way I reflect back upon it now:

"There's no place in this world where I'll belong when I'm gone
And I won't know the right from the wrong when I'm gone
And you won't find me singin' on this song when I'm gone
So I guess I'll have to do it while I'm here"

Finally, our discussion turned to Maharishi Mahesh Yogi, the famous "giggling guru". In an odd way, the fictional Cletus Underwood, Dr. Sipe believed, seemed to exemplify the Yogi's 1967 dictum that "Being happy is of the utmost importance…Just think of any negativity that comes at you as a raindrop falling into the ocean of your *bliss*." This turn in our discussion was vital. Before, with Duchamp and Ochs, we had been mostly flexing our muscles. But now, Dr. Sipe had turned things back to the heart of *Missing May*, in a way that made concrete Louise Rosenblatt's (1996) statement that "Knowledge of literary forms is empty without an accompanying humanity" (p. 51). For Dr. Sipe, as for Cletus, humanity was what it's ultimately all about. His perspective led my way to "new vistas of experience," and into thickly wooded jouissance.

It was in revisiting, over and over, this and other discussions I had with Dr. Sipe that I began to heal from his death. In a miraculous way, he played the roles both of Rylant's May *and* Cletus, as he was both the person I missed and the person who enabled me to grapple through my grief and into happiness again.

Dr. Sipe, you spoke with wisdom, and on your tongue there was tender instruction. You did so very much while you were here. You were *our* giggling guru. I hope you have your bliss, now and ever.

References

Ochs, Phil. (1966). When I'm Gone. On *Phil Ochs in Concert* [LP]. New York: Elektra.
Rosenblatt, Louise. (1996). *Literature as Exploration* (5th ed.). New York: The Modern Language Association of America. (Original work published 1938.)
Rylant, Cynthia. (1992). *Missing May*. New York: Scholastic.
Sipe, Lawrence R. (2008). *Storytime: Young Children's Literary Understanding in the Classroom.* New York: Teachers College Press.

Children's Literature in Education (2012) 43:51–71
DOI 10.1007/s10583-011-9156-x

COMMEMORATIVE ISSUE FOR DR. LAWRENCE SIPE

Exploring Grade 7 Students' Responses to Shaun Tan's *The Red Tree*

Sylvia Pantaleo

Published online: 15 February 2012
© Springer Science+Business Media, LLC 2012

Abstract As art objects, picturebooks have the potential to contribute to readers' aesthetic development. Many scholars and practitioners have recognized how using picturebooks with older students can augment their reading motivation and extend their understanding of visual elements of art and design, as well as develop their literacy, language, and thinking skills. The *Red Tree* (Tan, 2001) was one of the picturebooks used during two multifaceted, classroom-based research projects with Grade 7 students. The studies explored how the students responded to and interpreted picturebooks and graphic novels with metafictive devices, and examined how the students transferred their knowledge and understanding of various literary and art elements when creating their own multimodal print texts. Overall, the content analysis of the students' written responses to The *Red Tree* revealed an adoption of an "aesthetic attitude" (Doonan, Looking at Pictures in Picture Books, 1993, p. 11) towards the picturebook. The students' responses reflected how they positioned themselves as active readers who looked closely at Tan's sophisticated and metaphorical paintings, and who embraced a co-authoring role as they interpreted the emotional landscapes and textual fragments in the picturebook. The article concludes with a discussion of several pedagogical issues associated with using picturebooks in middle years' classrooms.

Keywords Picturebooks · Students' responses · Middle years

Sylvia Pantaleo is an Associate Professor in the Department of Curriculum and Instruction in the Faculty of Education at the University of Victoria, British Columbia, Canada. She teaches undergraduate and graduate courses in language and literacy, and children's literature.

S. Pantaleo (✉)
Department of Curriculum and Instruction, Faculty of Education, University of Victoria,
Box 3010 STN CSC, Victoria, BC V8W 3N4, Canada
e-mail: pantaleo@uvic.ca

Prologue

Larry Sipe was my good friend, colleague and picturebook soulmate. I feel privileged to have known and worked with Larry and regret not knowing him for longer than I did.

Larry had immense admiration for the teachers and young children who participated in his research. In *Storytime: Young Children's Literary Understanding in the Classroom* (2008a) Larry explained how he was "intrigued by young children's understanding and interpretation of stories" and fascinated by the children's "talk about the words and illustrations" in picturebooks (p. 1). This article is a tribute to Larry Sipe—to his commitment to conducting classroom-based research, to his deep love of picturebooks, to his beliefs that students' experiences with picturebooks should be aesthetic in nature and that picturebooks can develop students' literary understanding, and to his fascination with students' responses to picturebooks.

Introduction

In his 1991 Caldecott Medal acceptance speech, author and illustrator David Macaulay (1991) expressed great concern about "visual illiteracy" and "visual complacency," about people neither really "seeing what is going on around" them (p. 411) nor seeing "how things work" (p. 413). Macaulay stated that, "it is essential to see, not merely to look" (p. 419), and that "seeing necessitates looking and thinking" (p. 411). Echoing Macaulay's beliefs about the importance of "seeing," Elliot Eisner (2004, 2009) has discussed the need for and importance of slowing down perception. According to Eisner (2009),

> learning how to slow down perception is one of the primary ways in which one can enrich one's experience… [and that] much of human experience is dissipated or weak because of the absence of time that needs to be taken in order to see, to really see. (p. 8)

In my program of research, elementary and middle school students have participated in activities that have required them to "slow down perception" (Eisner, 2004, p. 5), and that have demonstrated to them the multiple benefits of "seeing" (Pantaleo, 2008, 2011a; Pantaleo and Bomphray, 2011). The students in my research have also received instruction that has informed their "savouring" of texts, their qualitative exploration of a variety of "qualities that constitute the qualitative wholeness of the object or event being perceived" (Eisner, 2009, p. 8). The "objects" that the student participants have had opportunities to learn about "seeing" and "savouring" have been picturebooks and graphic novels.

I believe that students need time to, as well as instruction about how to engage in deep reading and deep thinking in school. However, students also need access to texts (print and digital) that engage them as readers and that warrant both deep reading and deep thinking. *The Red Tree* by Tan (2001) was a selection of literature that was savoured and thought about deeply by two classes of Grade 7 students that I worked with during 2009. Tan (n.d.) has explained how the text in *The Red Tree* is "consciously minimal and prosaic so as not to get in the way of the mysterious invitation offered by each painting to the reader" (para. 23). Thus, Tan conveys great respect for various interpretations of his artwork by readers who are positioned in a co-authoring role. This article focuses on the Grade 7 students' written responses to *The Red Tree* and discusses how the students accepted and embraced Tan's invitation.

A discussion of the relevant literature and a brief overview of the guiding theoretical frameworks of the research are followed by a short explanation of the research procedures, and by the analysis and discussion of the students' written responses.

Picturebooks as Aesthetic Objects

According to Marantz (1977), a picturebook is an art object that "must be experienced as a visual-verbal entity if its potential values are to be realized" (p. 150). A picturebook, unless it is wordless, "hinges on the interdependence of pictures and words" (Bader, 1976, p. 1). Many scholars have theorized about the relationship between the mode of image and mode of writing in picturebooks. Some academics (e.g., Agosto, 1999; Doonan, 1993; Golden, 1990; Nikolajeva and Scott, 2001; Schwarcz, 1982) have developed schemes to portray the word-picture dynamic in picturebooks while others have used a single term/concept or metaphor to describe the text-picture relationship in picturebooks: Sipe (2008a) embraces the word synergy, and Mitchell (1994) uses the term "imagetext" (p. 9). Lewis (2001) takes on an ecological perspective that emphasizes "the interdependence or interanimation of word and image" (p. 48) in picturebooks. Regardless of descriptive scheme or term, the concept of transmediation, "a special case of semiosis in the sense that learners use one sign system to mediate another" (Siegel, 1995, p. 461), seems to accurately describe the relationship between the verbal and visual texts in picturebooks.

Embracing a semiotic perspective, Moebius (1986) has explained how meaning is conveyed in the visual text in picturebooks through five graphic codes that are "interactive, [and] simultaneous" (p. 151). Indeed, according to Sipe (2008a), "literary understanding of picturebooks includes learning to read the visual text of the illustrational sequence" (p. 18). As art objects, picturebooks are invaluable sources to develop students' "visual aesthetic understanding" (Sipe, 2008b, p. 131). Studies have revealed how students, regardless of their age, academic ability, or cultural or linguistic background, have articulated insightful interpretations of the artwork in picturebooks (Arizpe and Styles, 2003; Day, 1996; Kiefer, 1995; Sipe, 2008a; Walsh, 2003). For example, Arizpe and Styles (2003) used three multilayered picturebooks to investigate how children aged 4–11 read visual texts. They found that the children, who participated in individual and group interviews about the literature, were sophisticated readers of visual texts. The children "read colours, borders, body language, framing devices, covers, endpapers, visual metaphors and visual jokes" (Arizpe and Styles, 2003, p. 224). Maureen Walsh (2003), who also examined children's reading of visual texts, found that the images in picturebooks evoked a variety of insightful responses in the research participants, for some of whom English was a second language. Further, research that has focused on postmodern picturebooks and picturebooks with Radical Change characteristics (Dresang, 1999) has revealed students' engagement with, understanding of, and sophisticated responses to the artwork in these texts (Pantaleo, 2008; Sipe and Pantaleo, 2008).

Picturebooks and Middle Years Students

Several individuals have written about the potential of using picturebooks with older students (e.g., Ammon and Sherman, 1996; Benedict and Carlisle, 1992; Billman, 2002; Murphy, 2009; Pantaleo, 2010, 2011b; Roser et al., 2011). However, some teachers question the appropriateness of picturebooks as literature for their adolescent students, and some middle years students may hold misconceptions about picturebooks. Some teachers and students may not understand the opportunities offered by picturebooks to learn about literary theory, literary elements, and visual elements of art and design. Indeed, the artwork in picturebooks can be used in visual literacy instruction as students learn "how to analyze and interpret and compose and create images and visual communications" (Metros, 2008, p. 106). Numerous contemporary picturebooks explore abstract concepts, complex topics and mature themes. Further, the nature of several picturebooks with Radical Change and postmodern characteristics provides students with the kind of reading experiences that can develop their abilities to critically analyze, construct and deconstruct an array of texts and representational forms. Picturebooks can be used for teacher read-alouds, for student independent reading, for literature discussions, as "models for students' writing" (Martinez et al., 2009, p. 293), for critical literacy pedagogy, and for multidisciplinary instruction. Indeed, picturebooks have the potential to promote the development of student literacy, language, and thinking skills. In addition, I believe that it is fundamental for older readers to learn to approach, appreciate and examine picturebooks as aesthetic objects, as a "literary art form" (Tan, n.d., para. 3).

Embracing an Ecological Perspective

I was both a teacher and the researcher during the studies with the Grade 7 students. I acknowledge my influence on the classroom communities and specifically the students' learning. The "ideologies demonstrated and valued" (Rowe, 2008, p. 70) by both myself and Mrs. K., the classroom teacher, about literature, literacy and student learning, as well as the texts and the particular kinds of "textual practice[s]" (Dyson, 2001, p. 381) featured within the Grade 7 classrooms, influenced the students' stance toward the focus literature, the content of both the students' written work and their small group discussions, the nature of the students' contributions to whole class discussions, and the composition of their multimodal texts. The students' participation in daily and interdependent activities created a particular classroom "community of practice" (Lave, 1996). Adoption of a situated learning perspective recognizes "the polyphony of interaction" (Linehan and McCarthy, 2000, p. 439) in classrooms and the reciprocity of influence in socially structured practices. The students' ongoing learning affected their participation in the activities, including their discourse, my pedagogy, and the nature of learning in the research classrooms. Indeed, student engagement in the literacy and discursive practices offered during the research, which positioned the students as capable and active participants within the classroom communities (Davies and Harré, 1999), contributed to the students' evolving individual and collective identities.

Louise Rosenblatt's transactional theory (1978) explains how students' reading transactions are affected by the synergistic interplay of numerous personal, textual and contextual factors. Her ecological consideration of the literary transaction accounts for the particularity of reader evocation and the diversity of reader response. Rosenblatt also distinguishes aesthetic from efferent reading and views these two stances as forming poles of a continuum. Rosenblatt's transactional theory was foundational to my research with the Grade 7 students because the students were expected to approach the focus literature from a predominantly aesthetic stance, and to explore multiple interpretations of the picturebooks and graphic novels in their written work and during their conversations.

Consistent with the fundamental underpinnings of Rosenblatt's transactional theory, a sociocultural theory of writing frames students' writing as a "social practice that is local, positioned, and cultural" (Rowe, 2008, p. 69). Defining writing as a social practice recognizes the connections among the reading, talking and the writing engaged in by the students during the research, and the influence of their membership in a particular classroom community. The brief description of the research context below provides information about how the Grade 7 students' written responses to *The Red Tree* were affected by reading, writing about and discussing a particular collection of texts, engaging in activities and interacting with others, and receiving explicit instruction on various literary and illustrative concepts.

The Studies

The Research Context

The students whose written responses were analyzed for this article attended a Grades 6–8 public school located in a city in western British Columbia, Canada. The middle school's predominantly upper-middle class catchment area is both culturally and ethnically diverse. Two separate studies were conducted with Mrs. K., a teacher whom I had collaborated with on a previous research project. During the first study (hereafter referred to as Year 1), which was conducted from January–March, 2009, I worked with a class of Grade 7 students four mornings/week for approximately 360 min/weeks for 10 weeks. During the second study (hereafter referred to as Year 2), which was conducted from September to December, 2009, I worked with another class of Grade 7 students five mornings/week for approximately 390 min/week for 11 weeks.

Mrs. K. described the Grade 7 students' academic achievement in Reading and Writing as follows: 13 students—C (Satisfactory Performance), 18 students—C+ (Good Performance), 16 students—B (Very Good Performance), and three students—A (Excellent Performance). Five students were identified as having a learning disability and one participant was designated as ESL. Overall, the students in both classes were pleasant and kind to each other and they worked together well as a class and in small groups.

Research Purposes and Investigative Procedures

During both classroom-based studies, the students had opportunities to: develop their understanding and appreciation of picturebooks and graphic novels; extend their comprehension, interpretive, and creative skills as they discussed and responded to the literature; and apply their learning by designing their own multimodal print texts. Succinctly, the overall purposes of the studies were to explore how developing the students' knowledge of literary and illustrative elements affects their understanding, interpretation and analysis of picturebooks and graphic novels, as well as their subsequent creation of print texts. In addition to learning about various metafictive devices (Pantaleo, 2008; Waugh, 1984), the students were introduced to some visual elements of art and design, and to a few compositional elements of graphic novels. The brief overviews below offer only a glimpse of the richness and complexity of the teaching and learning activities that occurred during the studies. Further, minimal information is provided about several aspects of the research as the students' written responses are featured in this article.

Personal Response and the Picturebooks

Initial instruction in both studies focused on the notion of 'response.' Through a variety of activities (i.e., listening to musical segments, visualizing sights, imagining smells, recalling particular memories, and discussing local and world events), we discussed how humans are continually responding to multiple stimuli in their lives, and that there are various kinds of responses and ways to respond. Instructional activities were also dedicated to establishing student understanding of the qualities of a "good aesthetic response," qualities that were consistent with the expectations outlined in provincial curriculum documents (e.g., articulating one's opinions, emotions, thoughts about a text and giving supportive reasons/explanations). During both years of the research the students received oral and written scaffolding to support and assist them with their written responses, and although all of the students demonstrated growth in their response writing, most students needed continued encouragement and instructional guidance to extend their ideas and opinions. Finally, instructional time was devoted to establishing small group discussion guidelines.

As the focus picturebooks were read and discussed, issues of intertextuality and various peritextual elements and other features of picturebooks were introduced to and/or reviewed with the students. For most of the focus picturebooks, the students read the book independently, completed a written response, and engaged in peer-led, digitally recorded small group discussions. Following the discussions, the students participated in whole class activities that focused on various metafictive devices used in the literature. With respect to visual elements in art and design, the students participated in a small number of activities that provided them with opportunities to learn about a few semiotic resources of the mode of image including size, colour, shape, perspective (i.e., how to create depth and distance), point of view and line.

Subsequent to the picturebooks, the students read, discussed and responded to four graphic novels. Once all of the selections of literature had been read, the students completed a brief questionnaire. They identified their favourite book (picturebook or graphic novel), described how they read picturebooks, and wrote comments that could be conveyed to individuals who might not appreciate all of the knowledge that is required to read and understand graphic novels. Finally, the culminating activity of the research involved the students creating a multimodal text as an artifact of their learning.

Before outlining the pedagogical procedures used with *The Red Tree* and describing how the students' written responses were analyzed, a brief description of Tan's picturebook follows.

The Red Tree

Allegorical in nature, Shaun Tan's *The Red Tree*[1] is a sophisticated picturebook. The evocatively surreal artwork and minimal text capture and convey the power of depression. The intricate detail in the complex and collage-like illustrations necessitates both multiple viewings and close analysis as much of the artwork encapsulates subtle symbolism.

The picturebook's identical dust jacket and hard cover feature a young girl with orangey-red hair afloat in a paper hat/boat. Words on the hat/boat and the nature of the reflection of the girl and her craft, including the image of a single red leaf, stimulate compelling thoughts and emotions. The mottled grey front endpages, featuring a single brown leaf, establish the atmosphere for Tan's absorbing and thought-provoking picturebook. On the first frontispiece, the young girl is located in a field, standing on a stool with jumbled letters spewing from a megaphone that is raised to her mouth. The second frontispiece features a framed illustration of a grandfather clock in a field with letters from the previous page scattered about in the bottom one-third of the page. The face of the timepiece, comprised of one red leaf (at the top) and seven brown leaves, features a single hand poised to strike the hour of the red leaf.

The framed illustration on the recto of the first opening shows the girl awakening to brown leaves descending into her bedroom. A picture of a single red leaf hangs above the girl's bed and a small snail sits on her desk. Below the illustration the text reads, "sometimes the day begins with nothing to look forward to" (unpaginated). The recto of the second opening reveals another framed illustration of the girl's bedroom, now nearly half full of brown leaves. The textual fragment reads, "and things go from bad to worse." The girl exits her bedroom and over the next 11 openings, wanders through imaginary and dreamlike landscapes that portray hopelessness and isolation—double-page spreads show the girl followed by a

---

[1] Some of the content of the description of Tan's picturebook was first published in a review I wrote of *The Red Tree* in *CM Magazine: Canadian Review of Materials*, Vol. X, No. 18, May 7, 2004. Available at umanitoba.ca/outreach/cm/vol10/no18/theredtree.html.

repulsive enormous fish with bloodied-eyes, enclosed in a glass bottle wearing a scuba diving helmet, and counting aimlessly on the shell of a giant snail. These transfixing fantasies overwhelm the girl with feelings of despair and melancholy. As well as conveying emotions and thoughts associated with depression, the textual fragments that accompany the artwork communicate sophisticated themes such as search for identity, lost opportunities, and pressure to conform. However, a red leaf depicted in each of Tan's mixed-media visual compositions seems to represent hope, even in the darkest moments of gloominess and loneliness.

When the girl returns to her bedroom at the end of the day, the red leaf is no longer in the framed picture—it is on the floor and is "quietly waiting" for her. A page turn reveals that the leaf has blossomed into a red tree, full of light and hope. The girl smiles and readers are reminded of the power of renewal and encouragement. Although the final endpages have the same marbled appearance as the beginning endpages, the closing pages are predominantly red.

The Red Tree and two other picturebooks by Tan have recently been collected into one volume called Lost & Found (Tan, 2011). This 2011 publication of three picturebooks includes additional artwork and notes by both Shaun Tan and John Marsden.

Pedagogical Procedures

The Red Tree was read and discussed earlier in the sequence of focus picturebooks during Year 2. In my opinion, and based on our experiences with Tan's picturebook in Year 1, the nature of the artwork encourages students to apply and extend their understanding of visual elements of art and design. Indeed, the surreal artwork inspires multiple interpretations and the fragments of text and lack of connections among the illustrations promote exploration of manifold meanings. Therefore, we thought it was appropriate to have the students read and discuss The Red Tree earlier in the research during Year 2.

During both studies, once copies of The Red Tree had been distributed, the students were directed to carefully view the dust jacket and to share their observations and thoughts. I used open-ended questions to engage the students in conversation about the endpages and the two frontispieces. The focus of these initial conversations was to encourage the students to interpret Tan's images, to consider not only the content of the images but his use of colour, line, perspective and point of view. During both years the students were eager to share their ideas and opinions. Subsequently, the students were instructed to work their way through the picturebook, reminded to "see" not merely look, and encouraged to think deeply about the possible meanings of each double-page spread or single page.

As well as altering the order of the books, I changed pedagogical procedures from Year 1 to Year 2. Generally, during both studies, the students read the literature, wrote an individual response and then discussed the selection of literature in small groups. However, during Year 1, the students discussed The Red Tree in their small groups *before* writing a response to the book. The sequence of activities was changed because overall, the students seemed tentative to express their personal opinions and ideas in their writing. Mrs. K. and I wondered if the content of the students' written responses would improve if they had an opportunity to talk about the literature with peers before they wrote about the book in their response journals. However, in Year 2, the students followed the usual sequence: they read *The Red Tree*, wrote a personal response and then discussed the picturebook in small groups. During each year approximately 25–30 min were allocated for student response writing to Tan's picturebook.

Data Analysis and Findings

In a classroom "a student's response will be like an iceberg: only a small part will become apparent to the teacher" (Purves and Rippere, 1968, p. xiii). I recognize that the students' written responses provide a limited view of their transactions with, responses to and interpretations of *The Red Tree*.

Two student absences resulted in a data set of 48 written responses. To expedite data management and analysis, I typed each student's response, conventionalized only the spelling, and saved the work in a word processing file. Year 1 students wrote approximately 165 words/response and Year 2 students wrote approximately 200 words/response. The written work was analyzed qualitatively in order to discover the nature of the students' responses to *The Red Tree*. I read the students' responses multiple times in order to develop an overall impression of the content of the work. Inductive category development involved the creation of tentative categories as I read through the students' responses. Content analysis, a "method of making inferences from texts and making sense of these interpretations in a context surrounding the text," requires close reading of text (Hoffman et al., 2011, p. 30). Data analysis was iterative and multiple readings of the data resulted in both the revising and/or combining of some of the initial categories. Once the main categories were derived, the entire data set was reread to ensure that the deduced categories accurately reflected the content of the students' responses. As well as using various colours to highlight text segments that corresponded to specific categories, students' names were recorded under the categories that reflected the content of their work. A few categories had a very small number of students' names and segments of text.

The content analysis of the students' written work revealed that every student wrote about more than one central idea or topic in his/her response. Each of the following categories were evident in at least 10 of the 48 student responses: the description and/or interpretation of specific openings, the presence of the red leaf, the emotions expressed by the young girl, the emotions conveyed by the artwork, the overall meaning of the picturebook, the emotions experienced by the reader, the typographic experimentation used in *The Red Tree*, and the quality of Tan's artwork. Below, the aforesaid categories are discussed in descending order of frequency, and *excerpts* from the students' written responses are featured in order to share as many student voices as possible. All student names are pseudonyms.

Description and/or Interpretation of Specific Openings

Overall, the written responses of 42 students included descriptive and/or interpretive comments about the artwork and/or text of specific openings in *The Red Tree*.

All but six of the 42 student responses included interpretations of the openings that students chose to write about. In total, the students wrote about 13 different openings of the picturebook. Openings 10, 7, 6 and 4 are discussed below because these four openings were the focus of most students' written work.

Eleven students wrote about opening 10, a "board game" that features a "*Citysaurus*" (Rylan) dangling an hourglass and the girl holding a single die with unusual numbering. Most of the students focused on the meaning of the die in the girl's hands, and on the significance of the hourglass held by the appendages of the mechanical creature.

> Another amazing illustration is the picture where she's on a giant board game holding a huge dice. If you look closely you can see that the every side of the dice is a 6, so the outcome will be the same every time. It looks to me like the game is her life and the evil monster symbolizes all the terrible fates that she will, inevitably, be faced with in time. I think the border of this picture is the gameboard and all of the squares are bad, nothing is easy or fun. And there are no squares that symbolize shortcuts because life is tough, hard work and there are no shortcuts. There is a three-leaf clover, which I suppose is good, but no four-leaf clovers, no luck. (Stefinia)

> My other favourite page was with the robot Godzilla and the brick wall pathway. I think the dice represents the luck and chance of life, she is alone on the roof top city. (Blake)

> My other favourite page is the one that says, "terrible fates are inevitable." I like this page because it's kind of showing what she sees but she is still just walking down the sidewalk. Another point is that the monster made of buildings is holding an hourglass like it's counting down her fate. She is also carrying a dice, which shows that she might have a chance of getting out of it. (Morgan)

Ten students commented on opening 7. In each of the eight framed illustrations on opening 7, the point of view changes as Tan zooms out from an extreme close-up of the girl aimlessly marking tallies on a snail's shell to a distance shot of the girl atop of the snail. Although the opening is pale in intensity, Tan includes many words and phrases on the verso and recto and readers must look closely to discern the text.

> When I saw the page with the all the waiting (the snail page), it sort of scared me in a way and made me feel as if I were in a prison chamber with this girl and we are waiting and waiting but nothing happens. (Brianna)

> As she sits atop of the snail and counts, it shows how slow time shall move. The snail is the movement of time and how we all crawl through those days. "~~1111~~, ~~1111~~, 1111 wait path silence gap alone alone alone wait now alone" is a line I read in the book and for me it represents how we see no light, how we are surrounded by sad never-ending thoughts of how we are drowning in despair. (Isabella)

Opening 6 is predominated by colours of red and yellow. The artwork, which is pastiche in nature, is composed of paint and layered pieces of original drawings, other images, and bits of various types of text, some in languages other than English. Scraps from dictionary pages border the collage composition. The nine students who wrote about opening 6 focused on the emotional effects of the colours used for this opening, the typographic experimentation evident in the illustration, the pastiche nature of the artwork, and the congruency between the phrase on the page, "without sense or reason" and the content of the artwork.

> My favourite page was the one with all of the red and yellow. I was shocked when I saw it because the page before was very dark and dull. It was pretty hard to find the red leaf here because it blended in with the other shades of red. I really liked the typographic experimentation used here because of all the sizes of fonts. This illustration also made sense with the text. The pictures were all jumbled up and the text was "without reason or sense." The text for the book stood out so it wouldn't blend in with the background words. It gave me a surge of happiness to finally see a bright page after all those other dull ones. If I had to compare this page with the page before it, I would say that they both had equivalent detail but the bright page looked more detailed because it had lots of words everywhere. (Liam)

> In one of the illustrations with the bright red for colour, it made sense about how the small quote said "without sense or reason" because the picture had bits of words and the quote worked with the picture in some ways to make it work in the story. (Vanessa)

Overall, seven students wrote about opening 4. The setting is a rocky beach and the girl, wearing a scuba diving helmet, sits enclosed in a narrow-necked glass bottle. The fragment of text reads, "nobody understands." The seven students interpreted the artwork and text to be communicating the girl's overwhelming feelings of despair and helplessness.

> My absolute favorite picture is when the nameless girl is trapped in a bottle while she has an old-fashioned diver's helmet on her head. For me that means she is trapped in her own thoughts and they are getting worse as the bottle is filling up with water from the rain. (Isaiah)

> In the picture of her with the helmet in the bottle, I thought it meant that she had no way out. She didn't know how to feel or there's no way out, so why bother. The background in this picture explains a lot too. In the part where the bottle is, it is dark and grey but the other side is a light blue with whitish clouds. I also noticed that the red leaf is on the outside of the bottle and it's not in her view which could mean that she is depressed because in some of the other pictures her life is better, not exactly happy, but better than when the leaf isn't near here. (Payton)

> I think the best and most "powerful" opening in this book The Red Tree is the one where the person is trapped in a bottle with a helmet on her head. I believe this is the best opening because it strongly says that the girl is feeling trapped in her life, that she has nowhere to go. The helmet on her head means that she's trying to ignore everything, that she's trying to stick her head into the sand. (Kohen)

Although not addressing specific openings, 11 students wrote about peritextual elements in *The Red Tree*. The four students who commented about one of the frontispieces conveyed their interpretations of the significance of aspects of the artwork (i.e., the megaphone, the face of grandfather clock). With respect to the endpages, seven students shared their opinions about how Tan's choice of colours symbolized the atmosphere or mood of the story.

> I really thought the way Shaun Tan used a megaphone for the little girl on the first frontispiece was effective. I interpreted that picture to mean that even though she used a megaphone no one could hear or understand her and that all her words were all jumble. (Landon)

> On the second frontispiece I wonder if all the leaves are dead except the red one, and whether she is waiting for the day the hands of time will reach the red leaf, or if all the leaves were red and joyful, only to silently die when the hands of time passed them. (Stefinia)

> The endpages match the beginning of the story and the end of the story. For example, the first endpages are grey and dirty and have an upsetting atmosphere to them (like the beginning of the book). But the final endpages are bright red and glowing and have a happy atmosphere to them (like the end of the story). (Gina)

Presence of the Red Leaf

Many students wrote about the red leaf that is present in every opening (as well as on the dust jacket and the hard cover, and the two frontispieces). All but 2 of the 36 students who noted the red leaf's presence made inferences about the meaning of this intratextual image. Most of the students thought that the red leaf symbolized hope or happiness. However, Baxter wrote, "I think the red leaf represents her heart." and Blake stated that, "I think the red leaf is a symbol not of hope or defeat but of progression through a difficult situation and once it passed, the leaf bloomed into the tree." A few students believed that the red leaf's location on the page conveyed significance, as is evident in Payton's response above. Although the students in both classes had been introduced to the term "intratextuality" when we read and discussed *Willy the Dreamer* (Browne, 1997), 12 of the 13 students who used the term in their response when writing about the red leaf were participants in Year 1.

> The leaf was an intratextual connection because it was in every picture in the book. I think Shaun Tan used that red leaf throughout the whole book because

it was like that bit of light in the dark. All the pictures are mixed up and dark, somewhat sad actually, but the leaf is vibrant and colourful. That is why I think the leaf is a symbol of happiness. (Sydney)

While I read this book I began to understand the girl was very unhappy and depressed because of the words that were said and the pictures. She could not find what she was looking for and maybe what she was looking for was happiness, which I think was represented by the leaf. I noticed that the leaf was in every picture so what I think the leaf being in every picture meant was that what she was looking for was right there in front of her. What she needed to do was stop trying so hard to find it and stop waiting for it to come to her and it would just reveal itself to her. I'm thinking that's what the leaf represents because sometimes when you have a problem you should stop trying so hard and it just might reveal the answer to you, because at the end of the book when she seemed almost like she was give up right in front of her in her room she sawthe leaf and she was smiling. (Keira)

Emotions Experienced by the Main Character

Twenty-seven students, 16 in Year 1 and 11 in Year 2, wrote about the main character's emotions. Some students took a general approach and described the overall emotions that they thought the girl was experiencing. Other students' remarks were more specific in nature as they chose to focus on specific openings in the picturebook.

There's still colour in the pages but it reflects her mood of gloomy and unwanted. However, on the last page she is not depressed because she knows that she made it through her horrible day. (Jenna)

The pictures are all abstract paintings and I think that is what you need to show what this girl is feeling. All her pain, boredom and just plain depression literally came out of the book and gives you that heart-dropping feeling. (Isaiah)

Character's mouth   As noted in the section on pedagogical procedures, the Grade 7 students in Year 1 discussed *The Red Tree* in small groups prior to writing their responses. One of the questions the students discussed in their groups was as follows: "The last illustration is the only page where the girl is shown with a mouth. Discuss your ideas about the significance of the absence of the mouth in all of the illustrations but the last one." Analysis of the students' responses indicated that my question influenced the content of some students' responses: in Year 1, 10 of the 24 students remarked on Tan's choice not to show the girl with a mouth until the final opening but in Year 2, no students commented about this absent facial detail.

The 10 students all hypothesized reasons to explain why the paintings did not depict the girl's mouth. The students' conjectures included the girl having no emotions to express, and the girl feeling depressed and sad. Several of the

10 students speculated that only the last illustration showed the girl with a mouth because she finally experienced feelings of happiness when she saw the red tree in her bedroom.

> I wonder why the character doesn't have a mouth. I predict it is because she doesn't have a reason to smile. She really had no sense of happiness. In the book it was like she was waiting for the tree to grow. She didn't know what was going to happen but she knew something was. (Annkia)

> Another thing I noticed about the last page is that it's the only page where she has a mouth. I wonder why that is but I also have a thought. I think that all the drawings could have had a mouth but that would have shown more emotion than Shaun Tan would have liked. It also brings out how special it was to see a smile from her. (Jenna)

> The last picture of the girl explains a lot to me. There's a large tree in her room. In this illustration she has a smile. In the other illustrations she does not even have a mouth. The only way you could tell her feelings were by her body language, but in this picture you can tell how she is feeling. It's almost like she is happy because in the other pictures, there isn't really a sign of life but if you look at this one, it's as if she is so happy that something is living. (Payton)

Emotions Conveyed by the Artwork

Twenty students expressed interpretations of emotions that were conveyed by the artwork. Many made comments about how they found the artwork, in general, to be gloomy and sad. Sixteen of the students wrote specifically about Tan's use of colour.

> The colours of the endpages are different – at the beginning the colour grey is depressing and the final end pages are a bright, bold red that could mean that she is happy and more happy about life. (Vanessa)

> I also found it a little depressing because of the colour, It is almost always a bad colour of black, grey, brown and blue. (Riley)

> Most pages had dark, gloomy colours but the last one is very bright and cheerful. (Jade)

Overall Meaning of the Picturebook

The responses of 20 students included statements about the overall meaning of Tan's picturebook. Most of the students' interpretations were philosophical in nature. Further, many students wrote about positive themes that they believed to be conveyed in Tan's sophisticated picturebook. The four excerpts that follow demonstrate the students' thinking about the fundamental messages communicated in *The Red Tree*.

The book was pretty depressing but it's kind of saying don't waste your life, for even sometimes if it's dark, you can always make it as bright and happy as the sun. (Kaelin)

I think this book is trying to tell us that life has its ups and downs but everything will be o.k. in the end. I also think this book is about "the good and the bad" but mostly the bad. It's about who you want to be and how you want to be and where you want to be, and telling you that people have a choice. (Gina)

I think this book signifies the light at the end of a dark road. Everything will warm up in the end. (Blake)

I understand what message book The Red Tree is giving out: when things get really bad and they don't seem like they'll get any better, you have to keep thinking there's hope and it may take longer than you want it to but things will turn around. (Kaylee)

Emotions Experienced by the Reader

Ten of the 14 students who included statements about the emotions they experienced as they read the picturebook were from Year 2. Many of these students described how Tan's use of colour, as well as the characters' expressions contributed to their emotional responses.

What made this story so gloomy was all of the really dark pictures like the picture when it says, "The world is like a deaf machine" and all of the people in that picture look so miserable, like there's not meaning to life. That's why I found this book really dark and sad. (Cadan)

In the first picture it sort of gave me a cold wintry feeling because it isn't very bright and all the leaves are dead and brown. And then they all just fall on top of her and you can tell that it is going to be a bad day. The fish scares me because it is crying black liquid and it seems as though that if you were to walk into the fish's mouth that you would just disappear into darkness. (Brianna)

The Red Tree is one of the most mysterious books I have ever read. The book has its scary and sad sort of art form, like it's pastiche and oil pastel colouring. The reason why I'm talking so much about this page [opening 6] is because of the warm colours on it. This made the picture a little bit scary and lonely (even though there's a cat peeping its head out on the bottom left hand corner). And one last thing about this page on the bottom part of the verso it has a cruel and scary sentence saying, "Your friends are all the dullest dogs I know." That sentence gave me the goosebumps. (Santino)

Typographic Experimentation

Of the 13 students who wrote about Tan's use of typographic experimentation, 10 were participants in Year 1 of the research. The students wrote about the effectiveness of the typography and how the variation of typography contributed to the overall messages and emotions of particular openings.

> This book used lots of typographic experimentation. For example on the page with the snail Tan used many different fonts, sizes and it really showed how depressed she was. (Mischa)

> The typographic experimentation really suited the story and the girl. The first page did not start with a capital letter on the first word in the sentence because maybe since the girl isn't happy she feels that her story didn't deserve to be capitalized. (Oria)

> "Without sense or reason" goes well as you have random words, like history, dull dog, modes and many more scattered across the page, some in handwriting, others in printing, some cut out from magazines, others torn out of a dictionary. All of this was effective, as it made you think as to why it was there. (Madeline)

Discussion

Overall, the students' responses reflect the adoption of an aesthetic stance and aesthetic attitude towards *The Red Tree*. According to Doonan (1993), embracing an aesthetic attitude towards "a picture and, by extension, a sequence of pictures in a picture book … means *doing* something: being active," and engaging in what she refers to as close looking (p. 11). Similarly, Arizpe and Styles (2008), synthesizing the key findings from their review of research into children's responses to multimodal texts, note the need for students (and teachers) to "look closely" at texts and to reread texts (p. 369). The Grade 7 students' written responses reflect how they positioned themselves as active readers who looked closely at Tan's sophisticated and metaphorical paintings, and who embraced a co-authoring role as they interpreted the emotional landscapes and textual fragments in the picturebook. The students' reading experiences of Tan's enigmatic book were affected by several factors including their participation in brief lessons on visual elements of art and design, the emphasis on personal response in the classroom interpretive community, and the ideologies and expectations communicated by Mrs. K. and me. The students were expected, encouraged and given time to ponder and savour *The Red Tree*. The response excerpts reveal that the students were involved "emotionally and cognitively," that they embraced an attitude of open-mindedness, and that they made "deeper meaning" from Tan's picturebook (Doonan, 1993, p. 11).

Many of the written responses communicate the students' understanding of the potential for visual images to convey meaning. According to Sipe (2008b), "full literary understanding of picturebooks includes learning the conventions and principles of visual art, at least implicitly" (p. 19). Arizpe and Styles (2008) also explain how "an understanding of the interaction between word and image ... gives the reader insights into the creation of picture books and other works of visual art" (p. 369). They assert that it is crucial for teachers and students to learn the metalanguage or terms "to discuss visual aspects" in order to develop better understanding of texts (2008, p. 369). Instruction in visual analysis can develop students' understanding of their active role as readers and enhance their "appreciation for picturebooks and the professional work that goes into creating them" (Wolfenbarger and Sipe, 2007, p. 279). Indeed, students' personal, appreciative and critical interpretations of the artwork in picturebooks can be fostered and enhanced through instruction that focuses on "the visual meaning-making systems deployed in images" (Unsworth et al., 2005, p. 10). If "we see what we learn to see" (Sipe, 2008b, p. 18) then it is fundamental that students receive instruction about what and how to "see" and engage in activities that afford them practice to "see" in schools. As noted previously, the Grade 7 students received instruction about the metalanguage used to describe various peritextual features of picturebooks and about a few visual elements of art and design. This pedagogy, as is evident in the students' response excerpts, informed their visual analysis of and responses to *The Red Tree*, and contributed to their understanding of the symbiotic relationship between the modes of text and image in the picturebook.

During both studies with the Grade 7 students, Mrs. K and I worked to scaffold the students' abilities to both develop and successfully express a deep understanding, appreciation and interpretation of the literature that was read, written about and discussed in the classrooms. Like Allington (2006), we believe that when students demonstrate their thinking, they demonstrate their understanding. Writing can help students "think through what they want to express" (Galda and Beach, 2001, p. 69). Allington (2006), discussing the importance of engaging students in thoughtful literacy, noted that those "students who were more often asked to explain, discuss, or write about the texts they had read were also more likely to demonstrate" higher-order thoughtful literacy proficiencies (p. 119). The written work of the Grade 7 students shows evidence of 'higher-order literacy proficiencies' as they engaged thoughtfully with ideas, made connections, and interpreted symbolic and thematic messages in *The Red Tree*.

Through participation in classroom communities of practice, students "learn to respond to literature as they acquire various social practices, identities, and tools" (Galda and Beach, 2001, p. 66). Consistent with one of the key themes from the research on "successful approaches to school reform" in elementary and middle school reading, the Grade 7 students were provided with "complex thinking and motivating learning activities" (Taylor et al., 2011, pp. 602, 618). The nature of the picturebooks and graphic novels that were read and discussed by the students and the pedagogical activities engaged in by the students during the studies contributed to the development of student qualitative reasoning skills (i.e., exploring, attending and interpreting image) (Siegesmund, 2005).

Picturebooks should be included in the wide variety of reading materials that are made available to all students and used by teachers. Many individuals have written about the potential of using picturebooks with older students. According to Wolfenbarger and Sipe (2007), "many older readers in particular have limited access to the artistry and possibilities of active reading that picturebooks offer" (p. 278). The Grade 7 students' written responses communicate their active reading of and engagement with *The Red Tree*. Appropriate picturebooks for middle years students can be motivational and engaging reading material, and engagement has been identified as a fundamental variable in reading achievement. Many scholars have written about the importance of providing students with a broad range of interesting texts in school to foster student engagement (e.g., Biancarosa and Snow, 2006; Guthrie and Davis, 2003), thereby contributing to the development of student intrinsic motivation for reading.

As well as affording opportunities to engage in and develop a "range of high-level thought," the social conversation picturebooks "can engender should be reason enough to bring these books to all children" (Wolfenbarger and Sipe, 2007, p. 278). Although not the focus of this article, the transcripts of the small group discussions, which documented the students' collaborative talk, provided further evidence of the students' complex thinking about *The Red Tree* (Pantaleo, 2011c). Lyle's (2008) review of the research on collaborative talk revealed it to be a "key component of success in all existing models for teaching thinking skills" (p. 282). Indeed, research "has affirmed the importance of authentic talk about text in the development of sophisticated engaged readers" (Galda and Beach, 2001, p. 69). However, students need to be taught the discussion skills that will facilitate their engagement in productive conversations about picturebooks and other texts.

Conclusion

In classrooms, "what teachers say and do, the texts they choose [for students to read] and how they choose them, and the tasks they set for their students" affect the affective and cognitive dimensions of student identity and learning (Galda and Beach, 2001, p. 71). Eisner (2004) states that the "kinds of [student] minds [that] we develop are profoundly influenced by the opportunities to learn" that schools provide (p. 8). Picturebooks, which afford readers with "a highly sophisticated visual aesthetic experience" (Sipe, 2008a, p. 13), should be included in the learning opportunities offered in middle schools. Discussion and analysis of the "high quality of art and design in picturebooks" can affect students' developing sense of "visual aesthetics" as well as contribute to their literary understanding (Sipe, 2008a, p. 16). Indeed, Doonan (1993) writes about the "contribution the picture book can make to our aesthetic development" (p. 7).

Tan (n.d.) believes that picturebooks are for readers of all ages and should not "suffer from narrow preconceptions of audience" (para. 5). He states, "What matters are ideas, feelings and the pictures and words that build them.... What are the ways that something can be represented to most effectively invite us to think and ask questions about the world we live in?" (para. 6). *The Red Tree* did indeed "invite" the Grade 7 students to think and to question. Clea noted how, "The Red Tree was an interesting book that makes your mind ask many questions" and Kaylee wrote, "I like this book because it really works your mind." As is evident by the student work discussed in this article, picturebooks can provide middle school students with deep reading experiences that require them to be active readers who think deeply about image and text.

References

Agosto, Denise. (1999). One and Inseparable: Interdependent Storytelling in Picture Storybooks. *Children's Literature in Education, 30*(4), 267–280.
Allington, Richard. (2006). *What Really Matters for Struggling Readers: Designing Research-Based Programs* (2nd ed.). New York: Pearson Education Inc.
Ammon, Bette, & Sherman, Gale. (1996). *Worth a Thousand words: An Annotated Guide to Picture Books for Older Readers*. Englewood, CO: Libraries Unlimited.
Arizpe, Evelyn, & Styles, Morag. (2003). *Children Reading Pictures: Interpreting Visual Texts*. London: RoutledgeFalmer.
Arizpe, Evelyn, & Styles, Morag. (2008). A Critical Review of Research into Children's Responses to Multimodal Texts. In James Flood, Shirley Brice Heath, & Diane Lapp (Eds.), *Handbook of Teaching Literacy Through the Communicative and Visual Arts* (Vol. II, pp. 363–373). New York: Lawrence Erlbaum Associates.
Bader, Barbara. (1976). *American Picturebooks from Noah's Ark to The Beast Within*. New York: Macmillan.
Benedict, Susan, & Carlisle, Lenore. (1992). *Beyond Words: Picture Books for Older Readers and Writers*. Portsmouth, NH: Heinemann.
Biancarosa, Gina, & Snow, Catherine. (2006). *Reading Next—A Vision for Action and Research in Middle and High School Literacy: A Report to Carnegie Corporation of New York* (2nd ed.). Washington, DC: Alliance for Excellent Education.
Billman, Linda. (2002). Aren't These Books for Little Kids? *Educational Leadership, 60*(3), 48–51.
Browne, Anthony. (1997). *Willy the Dreamer*. Cambridge, MA: Candlewick Press.
Davies, Bronwyn, & Harré, Rom. (1999). Positioning and Personhood. In Rom Harré & Luk van Langenhove (Eds.), *Positioning Theory: Moral Contexts of Intentional Action* (pp. 32–52). Oxford: Blackwell.
Day, Karen. (1996). The Challenge of Style in Reading Picturebooks. *Children's Literature in Education, 27*(3), 153–166.
Doonan, Jane. (1993). *Looking at Pictures in Picture Books*. Stroud: The Thimble Press.
Dresang, Eliza. (1999). *Radical Change: Books for Youth in a Digital Age*. New York: The H. W. Wilson Company.
Dyson, Anne Haas. (2001). Introduction … and a Warning. *The Elementary School Journal, 101*(4), 379–383.
Eisner, Elliot. (2004). What can Education Learn from the Arts About the Practice of Education? *International Journal of Education & the Arts, 5*(4), 1–12.
Eisner, Elliot. (2009). What Education can Learn from the Arts. *Art Education, 62*(2), 6–9.
Galda, Lee, & Beach, Richard. (2001). Response to Literature as a Cultural Activity. *Reading Research Quarterly, 36*(1), 64–73.
Golden, Joanne. (1990). *The Narrative Symbol in Childhood Literature: Explorations in the Construction of Text*. Berlin: Mouton.
Guthrie, John, & Davis, Marcia. (2003). Motivating Struggling Readers in Middle School Through an Engagement Model of Classroom Practice. *Reading & Writing Quarterly, 19*(1), 59–85.
Hoffman, James, Wilson, Melissa, Martinez, Ramon, & Sailors, Misty. (2011). Content Analysis: The Past, Present, and Future. In Nell Duke & Marla Mallette (Eds.), *Literacy Research Methodologies* (2nd ed., pp. 28–49). New York: The Guilford Press.
Kiefer, Barbara. (1995). *The Potential of Picturebooks: From Visual Literacy to Aesthetic Understanding* Englewood Cliffs, NJ:Prentice-Hall, Inc.
Lave, Jean. (1996). Teaching, as Learning, in Practice. *Mind, Culture, and Activity, 3*(3), 149–164.

Lewis, David. (2001). *Reading Contemporary Picturebooks: Picturing Text* New York:RoutledgeFalmer.
Linehan, Carol, & McCarthy, J. (2000). Positioning in Practice: Understanding Participation in the Social World. *Journal for the Theory of Social Behaviour, 30*(4), 435–453.
Lyle, Susan. (2008). Learners' Collaborative Talk. In Nancy Hornberger, Marilyn Martin-Jones, & Anne-Marie de Mejia (Eds.), *Encyclopedia of Language and Education: Volume 3: Discourse and Education* (2nd ed., pp. 279–290). New York: Springer.
Macaulay, David. (1991). Caldecott Acceptance Speech. *Horn Book Magazine, 67*(4), 410–421.
Marantz, Kenneth. (1977). The Picture Book as Art Object: A Call for Balanced Reviewing. *Wilson Library Bulletin, 52*(2), 148–151.
Martinez, Miriam, Roser, Nancy, & Harmon, Janis. (2009). Using Picture Books with Older Learners. In Karen Wood & William Blanton (Eds.), *Literacy Instruction for Adolescents: Research-based Practices* (pp. 287–306). New York:The Guilford Press.
Metros, Susan. (2008). The Educator's Role in Preparing Visually Literate Learners. *Theory into Practice, 47*(2), 102–109.
Mitchell, William J.T. (1994). *Picture Theory: Essays on Verbal and Visual Representations.* Chicago: University of Chicago Press.
Moebius, William. (1986). Introduction to Picturebook Codes. *Word and Image, 2*(2), 141–158.
Murphy, Patricia. (2009). Using Picture Books to Engage Middle School Students. *Middle School Journal, 40*(4), 20–24.
Nikolajeva, Maria, & Scott, Carole. (2001). *How Picturebooks Work.* New York: Garland Publishing.
Pantaleo, Sylvia. (2008). *Exploring Student Response to Contemporary Picturebooks.* Toronto: University of Toronto Press.
Pantaleo, Sylvia. (2010). Contemporary Picturebooks with Radical Change Characteristics. In M.C. Courtland & T. Gambell (Eds.), *Literature, Media, and Multiliteracies in Adolescent Language Arts Classrooms* (pp. 103–125). Vancouver, BC: Pacific Educational Press.
Pantaleo, Sylvia. (2011a). Grade 7 Students Reading Graphic Novels: "You Need to do a lot of Thinking". *English in Education, 45*(2), 113–131.
Pantaleo, Sylvia. (2011b). Middle Years Students' Collaborative Talk About The Red Tree: "A Book That Works Your Mind". *Australian Journal of Language and Literacy, 34*(3), 260–278.
Pantaleo, Sylvia. (2011c). WARNING: A Grade 7 Student Disrupts Narrative Boundaries. *Journal of Literacy Research, 43*(1), 39–67.
Pantaleo, Sylvia, & Bomphray, Alexandra. (2011). Exploring Grade 7 Students' Written Responses to Shaun Tan's *The Arrival. Changing English: Studies in Culture and Education, 18*(2), 173–185.
Purves, Alan, & Rippere, Victoria. (1968). *Elements of Writing About a Literary Work: A Study of Response to Literature.* Research Report No. 9. Urbana, IL: National Council of Teachers of English.
Rosenblatt, Louise. (1978). *The Reader, the Text, the Poem: The Transactional Theory of the Literary Work.* Carbondale, IL: Southern Illinois University Press.
Roser, Nancy, Martinez, Miriam, & Fowler-Amato, Michelle. (2011). The Power of Picturebooks: Resources That Support Language and Learning in Middle Grade Classes. *Voices from the Middle, 19*(1), 24–31.
Rowe, Deborah. (2008). Social Contracts for Writing: Negotiating Shared Understandings About Text in the Preschool Years. *Reading Research Quarterly, 43*(1), 66–95.
Schwarcz, Joseph. (1982). *Ways of the Illustrator: Visual Communication in Children's Literature.* Chicago: American Library Association.
Siegel, Marjorie. (1995). More Than Words: The Generative Power of Transmediation for Learning. *Canadian Journal of Education, 20*(4), 455–475.
Siegesmund, Richard. (2005). Teaching Qualitative Reasoning: Portraits of Practice. *Phi Delta Kappan, 87*(1), 18–23.
Sipe, Lawrence R. (2008a). *Storytime: Young Children's Literary Understanding in the Classroom.* New York: Teachers College Press.
Sipe, Lawrence R. (2008b). Young Children's Visual Meaning Making in Response to Picturebooks. In James Flood, Shirley Brice Heath, & Diane Lapp (Eds.), *Handbook of Teaching Literacy Through the Communicative and Visual Arts* (Vol. II, pp. 381–391). New York: Lawrence Erlbaum Associates.
Sipe, Lawrence R., & Pantaleo, Sylvia (Eds.). (2008). *Postmodern Picturebooks: Play, Parody, and Self-Referentiality.* New York: Routledge.
Tan, Shaun. (2001). *The Red Tree.* Melbourne:Lothian.

Tan, Shaun. (2011). *Lost & Found*. Melbourne: Arthur A. Levine Books.
Tan, Shaun. (n.d.). *Picture Books: Who are They for?* Accessed February 1, 2009, from http://www.shauntan.net/comments1.html
Taylor, Barbara, Raphael, Taffy, & Au, Kathryn. (2011). Reading and School Reform. In Michael Kamil, P. David Pearson, Elizabeth Moje and Peter Afflerbach (Eds.), *Handbook of Reading Research* (Vol. IV, pp. 594–628). New York: Routledge.
Unsworth, Len, Thomas, Angela, Simpson, Alyson, & Asha, Jennifer. (2005). *Children's Literature and Computer Based Teaching*. Berkshire: Open University Press.
Walsh, Maureen. (2003). 'Reading' Pictures: What do they Reveal? Young Children's Reading of Visual Texts. *Reading: Literacy and Language, 37*(3), 123–130.
Waugh, Patricia. (1984). *Metafiction: The Theory and Practice of Self-Conscious Fiction*. New York: Methuen.
Wolfenbarger, Carol, & Sipe, Lawrence R. (2007). A Unique Visual and Literary Art Form: Recent Research on Picturebooks. *Language Arts, 84*(3), 273–280.

Children's Literature in Education (2012) 43:72–73
DOI 10.1007/s10583-011-9152-1

COMMEMORATIVE ISSUE FOR DR. LAWRENCE SIPE

Retelling and Remembering: In Honor of Dr. Lawrence Sipe

Danielle Gioia

Published online: 15 February 2012
© Springer Science+Business Media, LLC 2012

Abstract One of four personal reflections from doctoral students at the University of Pennsylvania Graduate School of Education that highlight Dr. Sipe, the teacher, whose love of the classroom and his students has left a hole in the academic community that cannot be filled.

Keywords Dr. Sipe · Tribute · Memorial · Reflections

Dr. Sipe illuminated so much about the way children talk and think about literature. It is unsurprising that one of his most powerful gifts was how he himself talked about children.

On the first page of his book *Storytime* (2008), Dr. Sipe recalls a kindergarten student, Keyron, who responded to his teacher's question about Red Riding Hood's premise with what he calls a triple pun: "Probably she read and she write a lot, and she live in the hood!" (p. 1). I vividly remember the time Dr. Sipe shared this story with me during a meeting. Reciting it verbatim, he marveled at the sophistication, quickness, and playfulness of Keyron's pun. Despite having beautifully captured this story about Keyron in his book, Dr. Sipe saw it as a story that demanded retelling. There was so much pleasure and learning alike to be gained and shared each new time.

Danielle Gioia is a third year doctoral student in the Reading/Writing/Literacy program at the University of Pennsylvania's Graduate School of Education. Before attending GSE, Danielle earned an MA in English literature at Tufts University, where she also completed all doctoral coursework in English literature. She holds a BA in English literature and studio art from Wheaton College in Norton, MA.

D. Gioia (✉)
Graduate School of Education, Reading/Writing/Literacy Program, University of Pennsylvania, 3700 Walnut Street, Philadelphia, PA 19104, USA
e-mail: dgioia@dolphin.upenn.edu

 Springer

The sheer delight with which he retold this striking triple pun was irrepressible. And the esteem in which he so clearly held young readers like Keyron—his belief in the power and potential of their imagination—was ever-present in his teaching. Children were always at the center of our class discussions, whether he was helping us delve into picture books or research design. He sometimes read to us, too, opening up unforgettable spaces for our own readerly selves to dwell. The indelible "experience of 'story'" (Sipe 2008, p. 247) that Dr. Sipe made possible for us contains a profound and enduring story about his teaching, as well, with so much left to learn, remember, and retell.

Reference

Sipe, Lawrence R. (2008). *Storytime: Young Children's Literary Understanding in the Classroom.* New York: Teachers College Press.

Children's Literature in Education (2012) 43:74–85
DOI 10.1007/s10583-011-9154-z

COMMEMORATIVE ISSUE FOR DR. LAWRENCE SIPE

Towards a Culturally Situated Reader Response Theory

Wanda Brooks · Susan Browne

Published online: 15 February 2012
© Springer Science+Business Media, LLC 2012

Abstract This article describes a theory of how culture enables literary interpretations of texts. We begin with a brief overview of the reader response field. From there, we introduce the theory and provide illustrative participant data examples. These data examples illustrate the four cultural positions middle grade students in our research assumed when responding to salient textual features embedded in African American children's novels. Our theory suggests that because a range of cultural positions factors into students' meaning making, we should mine

---

Wanda M. Brooks is an Associate Professor of Literacy Education in the College of Education at Temple University. She teaches graduate and undergraduate courses related to literacy theories and instruction. Dr. Brooks' primary research interest consists of examining the literary interpretations of African American middle school youth who read children's and young adult multicultural literature. She has published in journals such as *Reading Research Quarterly*, *Children's Literature in Education*, and *The Journal of Adolescent and Adult Literacy*. Her most recent book, co-edited with Jonda McNair, is titled: *Embracing, Evaluating and Examining African American Children's and Young Adult Literature*. Prior to becoming a university professor, Dr. Brooks taught middle grades in several public schools.

Susan Browne is an Associate Professor in the department of Language, Literacy, and Special Education at Rowan University. She teaches undergraduate and graduate reading courses, chairs the undergraduate reading endorsement program and serves as a research advisor to Master's and doctoral candidates. In the city of Camden, she has served as a university liaison with a pre-kindergarten through eighth grade school where she provided literacy support across the grades. Formerly a School District of Philadelphia classroom teacher, she remains active in the city as a Teacher Consultant for the Philadelphia Writing Project and coordinator of the Children of the Sun Literary Club at Bushfire Theatre of Performing Arts. Dr. Browne's research interests are in the areas of multicultural literature, reader response, critical and new literacies. Her publications for Scarecrow Press and the Journal of Adult and Adolescent Literacy address middle school students' response to multicultural literature.

W. Brooks (✉)
Temple University College of Education, 1301 Cecil B. Moore Avenue, RH 449, Philadelphia, PA 19122, USA
e-mail: wbrooks@temple.edu

S. Browne
Rowan University, Glassboro, NJ, USA

 Springer

texts more carefully for cultural milieu as well as find acceptance with a broader range of literary interpretations. We conclude by discussing implications for literary researchers and practitioners who study or use multicultural children's literature.

Keywords Reader response theory · Literary interpretation · Culture

While students in Dr. Lawrence Sipe's *Responding to Literature* class at the University of Pennsylvania, we often had to write journal entries in response to the children's and young adult literature read in the course. Susan Browne (2nd author) wrote one such journal following our reading of *Zeely* by Hamilton (1967). The book holds the distinction of being one of the first highly regarded African American children's novels. It tells the story of brother and sister, Elizabeth and John Perry's summer visit to their Uncle Ross' farm. As their trip begins, the characters transform themselves into Geeder and Toeboy. During Geeder's coming of age summer, she takes a journey of rewarding self discovery after meeting Zeely, whom she believes to be a Watusi queen.

During a class sharing of responses to the text, a White American classmate mentioned that she found ending the story with Geeder talking about eating a sweet potato an odd way for Hamilton to conclude the novel. The book ends in the following way:

> She was hungry again, as she usually was soon after supper. Maybe Uncle Ross had saved her a sweet potato.
> "I only had one," she said. "I was talking so much, I didn't even taste it" (p. 122).

Here is Susan's journal response to the same passage.

> November, 17. 1996
> I have been giving more thought to *Zeely* and the way the book ended. I've come up with the idea that Geeder's closing reference to sweet potatoes is deeply embedded in culture and symbolic of her rite of passage. The sweet potato and its cousin the yam are cross continental culinary staples with deep roots in African and African American cultures. This reference to the sweet potato seems to reinforce the relationship between Geeder and Zeely, Africa and America and Geeder's new depth of understanding. Feminist author, bell hooks, points to the yam as a unifier in her book, *Sisters of the Yam: Black Women and Self-Recovery* (1993). The sweet potato and the yam point to the discourse of feeling. Geeder has come of age and her desire to eat her sweet potato is another way of pointing that out.

Since taking the *Responding to Literature* Course and completing our dissertations under the tutelage of Dr. Sipe almost a decade ago, as African American scholars we have been thinking about and researching the puzzlement highlighted above (two very different understandings of the same book ending). However, unlike this graduate school example, our inquiries focus on middle grades African American readers and their interpretations of one sort of multicultural text, African American.

Our lines of research examine the ways literary interpretations are influenced by readers' ethnic backgrounds as well as the cultural milieu embedded in the stories they read.

Since embarking on this line of research over a decade ago, we have longed for culturally based reader response theories that might inform the analysis of our study participants' textual interpretations. In the years following our course, Dr. Sipe often encouraged us to develop grounded theoretical models from our dissertation studies and to further build on leading response theorists to better understand how culture enables literary response. This manuscript represents our development of such a theory. Throughout, we rely on data from a previous study about middle grade youth interpretations of children's books to introduce a culturally situated reader response theory. We begin with a brief overview of the reader response field. From there, we introduce the theory and provide illustrative participant response examples to exemplify the theory's tenets. We conclude by discussing implications for literary researchers and practitioners who study or use children's literature.

Brief Overview of the Reader Response Field

Reader response scholars rely on individual interpretations of books to make the literary understandings constructed throughout the reading process visible. These scholars situate children (and everything influencing their identities) in very active roles as readers (Beach, 1993; Tompkins, 1980). Despite their common goal, response theorists foreground modes of interpretations differently and across a wide continuum (See, Sipe, 2008, *Storytime*, chapters 2–3 for fuller discussion of types of reader response theories briefly summarized below.)

In general, it makes sense to organize these theorists in three broad categories. First, there is a group who privilege authors by foregrounding the construction of the genre and features of the particular narratives the authors attempt to tell (Rabinowitz, 1987). While still giving the reader an active role, these theorists pay most attention to the ways in which authors guide interpretation through a particular set of literary conventions. Still, even within this end of the continuum, it's likely that "different readers will naturally and inevitably construct different meanings of the same text" (Sipe, 2008, p. 50).

On the opposite end of the continuum exist scholars who assert that the text itself has very little to do with one's interpretation of meaning. Despite the content or nature of the written words, readers create unique understandings of stories. Each person carries out his or her own very subjective reading, and arriving at similar meanings is a result of the individuals not the material itself. Bleich's earlier work (1976), for example, suggests that literary interpretation is largely a result of someone's personality/psychology. He rarely refers to the supposed meaning embedded within the literature because this meaning plays only a small role in determining a reader's textual understanding. According to Bleich, the following factors greatly influence response: "age, sex, size, family situation, race, income and other things" (1976, p. 465).

Finally, as a middle ground, some theorists depict reading as a negotiation between both the text and the person engaging in the literary interpretation (Rosenblatt, 1982). From this point of view, what gets considered is how each (reader and text) influences the other during any construction of meaning. Rosenblatt (1982) stands out as one of the earliest scholars who strikes this middle ground. In short, she argues that reading occurs as, "a transaction, a two way process involving a reader and a text at a particular time, under particular circumstances" (p. 268).

A Culturally Situated Reader Response Theory

Although varied response theorists offer useful insights into how literary interpretations occur, we argue that few appreciably grapple with the myriad cultural influences (values, practices, experiences, etc.) affecting both readers and authors, and the ways in which these influence meaning making. Instead, most of the complicating factors such as age, gender, ethnicity, social contexts, or racial backgrounds get grouped together and mentioned merely in broad strokes by response theorists, if at all. Rosenblatt, for instance, does not specifically discuss readers in relationship to their ethnic backgrounds. She generally attends to the myriad experiences (physical, personal, social, and cultural) that cause readers to perceive their lives in unique ways (1982). In one of her few implicit references to culture, Rosenblatt maintains, "In order to shape [interpret] the work, we draw on our reservoir of past experiences with people and the world [culture]" (1982, p. 270).

Even though the above theories (and others) offer useful insights that help scholars analyze reader responses given by ethnically diverse youth, these theories are limited. As far as we can determine, a culturally situated reader response theory emerging from extensive data compiled from ethnically diverse readers and multicultural books does not exist. Cai's (2002) theoretical model encompasses dimensions of the cognitive, affective and social-communal as an overlapping set of concentric circles. This theory comes the closest to a theoretical response model that prioritizes culture because it addresses how culture might influence a particular dimension of the reading process. This model, though, pays little attention to the cultural milieu embedded in the books being read.

Below we describe a grounded theory (Strauss and Corbin, 1998) situated within the context of cultural practices and students' responses to multicultural literature. Parts of this grounded theory emerged from our dissertation studies, and we have continued to flesh out its applicability in our most recent research (i.e., Brooks, 2006; Browne and Brooks, 2008). This theory resides in the middle ground of the response theory spectrum. We privilege both readers and texts equally and in transactional ways. We build from reader interpretations of salient textual features embedded in novels written by and about African Americans such as recurring cultural themes, ethnic group practices and distinct linguistic styles. This theory, however, does not merely apply to African American youth and literature. It can address readers from all ethnic backgrounds. We use "African American" as a case

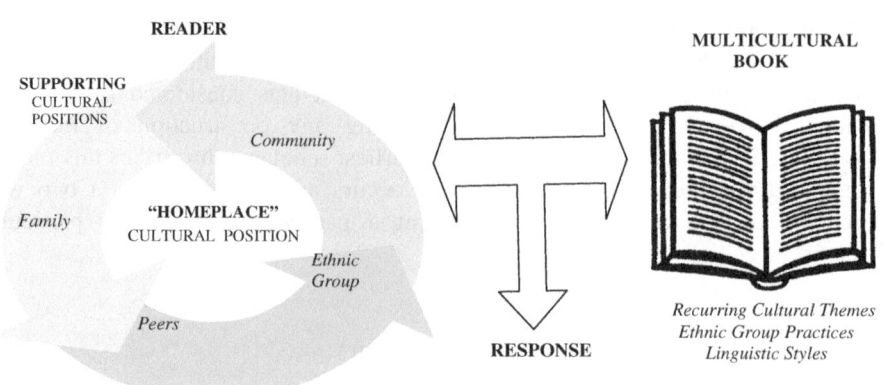

Fig. 1 "Homeplace": culturally situated reader response model

to illustrate how culture gets mediated between readers and narratives. Specifically, the response examples explored below derived from a study in which African American pre-adolescents read historical fiction novels, like *The Watsons Go to Birmingham – 1963* (Curtis, 1995), in a community-based literary club. Students also read novellas by Mildred Taylor such as her 1987 text, *The Friendship*. Written and oral responses were solicited for each book read.

The model above (see Fig. 1) highlights the cultural positions students assume while reading specific parts of stories. The Homeplace Position represents the most dominant perspective being evoked when a child offers a literary response. This position remains transient and constantly interacts with and gets informed by the other positions. The Supporting Positions continue to be influential to a student's response, but they are not as focal. These positions, moreover, cannot be fully grasped without taking into account the cultural milieu embedded in particular stories. For example, a book with a strong family theme (such as *Scorpions* by Walter Dean Myers, 1988) has been shown to compel participants to more often respond from a Family rather than an Ethnic Group positioning (Brooks, 2003).

Homeplace

As a foundation for our theory, Hooks (1990) discusses the importance of a place to call "home" for having a sense of self, personhood and identity. Through this lens, "home" embodies considerations for what it means to be an African ancestored individual and in this same way hooks' conception of "homeplace" can be understood as a meaning laden phenomenon with significant social and cultural dimensions. These dimensions emerge in the data through types of responses that led to our readers assuming four cultural positions when making sense of the books read. We've labeled these positions as: Ethnic Group, Community, Family and Peers. The positions emanating from what is termed as "Homeplace" occurred when readers identified themselves in four culturally specific ways in relationship to the text. It was in this Homeplace that the reader derived a focal cultural position. Collectively, these positions represent various multilayered aspects of one's culture and the multitude of practices inherent within it. The positions do not emerge as mutually exclusive or static. Rather, the positions are fluid, interactive and relied upon to make sense of unique situations embedded in the texts.

The Importance of Texts

As revealed in recent research, (Louie, 2006; Walach, 2008), we argue that textual features embedded in ethnically diverse books should not be ignored even when respecting the reader's role in constructing meaning. According to past scholarship on African American children's literature, authors insert particular cultural markers into these narratives. The fabric within the stories helps to identify this literature as written by and about African Americans (Bishop, 2007). Sims carried out a landmark investigation in this area in 1982. In her research on the history and types of African American children's literature created since the 1960s, she classified the books examined in one of the following ways: socially conscious, melting pot and culturally conscious. In general, the themes and ethnic-group depictions in these books accounted for the categorizations created by Sims. More recently, Bishop has reviewed several decades of children's writing by and about African Americans. She explains the now carefully documented literary tradition in the following way:

> For African American writers and artists who create children's books, embracing that freedom has resulted in a body of literature that holds within it a good deal of diversity as well as a number of important commonalities that serve to make it a distinctive body of work....African American children's books also often reflect or are influenced by the life experiences of their creators, and African American life and culture are far from monolithic. Nevertheless, the creators of African American children's literature all share the experience of being members of a society in which race matters a great deal more than it should....My assumption is that this shared concord of sensibilities, this eccentricity, this uneasy ideological difference, shapes the lenses through which Black authors and illustrators of children's books view their work and their worlds, and helps to coalesce their work in a canon of African American children's literature. (2007, Introduction, pp. xi–xii)

Other scholars with an expertise in African American children's literature have also written about distinct textual features that provide rich and authentic cultural depictions (Harris, 1990; Johnson, 1990; McNair, 2008; Rountree, 2008; Smith, 2001). Developing a theory such as this one compels us to consider the messages found within African American children's stories as a means of validating them as tools that pass on traditions, beliefs, histories, and values to upcoming generations of children (Gates, 1989, pp. 9–17).

Reader Responses from *The Watsons Go to Birmingham*

Within this section of the article, we rely on African American middle grades students' literature discussions in response to *The Watsons Go to Birmingham – 1963* by Christopher Paul Curtis to illustrate the culturally specific characteristics of each of the four response positions: Ethnic Group, Community, Family and Peers. A brief explanation of each positioning follows a summary of the novel.

The culturally conscious young adult novel, *The Watsons Go to Birmingham*, is told through the voice of middle child Kenny and presents strong themes around race and culture. Specific family themes that reoccur in children's writing by and about African Americans come in the forms Harris (1992) describes as "(1) families and their loyalties and obligations to each other and (2) the strength of the extended family" (pp. 73–74). The theme of confronting and overcoming racism is likewise present in this novel. When the shenanigans of oldest child Byron become too much for the family to withstand, a family trip south is planned. This culturally based tradition of transplanting the young from the north to the south is understood as an opportunity to purge problems through a connection or reconnection with one's history. The historical fiction text "acknowledges and reflects the distinctiveness of culture" (Bishop, 2007, p. 27). This is powerfully evident when the Watsons bear witness to the tragic Ku Klux Klan bombing of the Sixteenth Street Baptist Church and killing of four little girls. Kenny travels inside the bombed church and fears that he sees his younger sister injured. Brothers Kenny and Byron help each other put their lives back together from an event that has left them forever changed.

Ethnic Group Position

First, we categorize the Ethnic Group position by the manner in which students rely on who they are as ethnic beings with a particular historical status and lineage in the world at large and United States in particular. It refers to their broad identification as African Americans, so to speak. The Ethnic Group position captures how the youth viewed themselves as African Americans and internalized what an African American would do or believe. In the discussion that follows, an Ethnic Group position emerges in response to the recurring textual theme of confronting and overcoming racism woven throughout the narrative.

Malik: So why did they [the Ku Klux Klan, white people] hate black people so much that they didn't want you to go to the same school?
Cameron: Because we were their competition in everything.
Tia: Yeah, and because they [text characters] were black.
Cameron: It's like so many people suffered for what we have today.

From the Ethnic Group position, the children's talk of the 'we' was grounded in the language of seeking and offering rationale for what happened in the past and sharing historical knowledge. From there, the discussion intensified and spiraled into many directions having to do with ethnicity that included current interactions with what the participants perceived as rude sales clerks, teachers and police officers demonstrating cultural bias as well as deep understanding of their own collective as well as subjective position within US society. Cameron's response, "It's like so many people suffered for what we have today" speaks to how the text is indeed a cultural tool that transmits information about one's ethnicity in its broadest sense.

Community Position

Next, the Community position surfaced as a result of the students' immersions in an urban environment. This environment consists of various types of institutions (i.e., churches, mosques, schools, fast food restaurants, corner stores, etc.). A series of responses emerged after reading the following passage in the text about a remorseful Byron (the older brother in the story) who throws cookies at a bird:

> The cookie popped the bird smack-jab in the chest!
> When I got to Byron he'd picked up the bird and was holding it in his hands.
> You got him! You got him!
> I looked right at By and his face was all twisted up and his eyes were kind of shut.
> I stood there with my mouth open, I couldn't believe Byron was starting to cry. (Curtis, 1995, p. 81)

In the upcoming dialogue, the image that the protagonist Byron portrays in the text is discussed in relationship to images in the groups' immediate community.

Jerome: When he [Byron] killed the bird and started crying that means that he can be all tough on the outside. It's like an orange or a pineapple. It's all rough or hard on the outside, but then it's soft on the inside.

Cameron: Well Byron, right, he kind of resembles you know the image that people want today. The ironic part is that he killed a bird and feels sorry for it…

The Community position can be seen as the children use urbanized understandings to compare character image and persona with realities of their own community. A deeper sensibility surfaces as their talk points to understandings of socially constructed community understandings.

Tia: Killing something is different than beating somebody up.

Jerome: Yeah like when my friend Dwayne got shot. Tyree shot him. He's old, but he's about Tia's size. He's all right [Dwayne]. It was an accident. Tyree used to fight a lot, but when he shot him, he was like Dwayne! Oh my God!

In the textual moment that stands out for the readers, author Christopher Paul Curtis skillfully juxtaposes *wrong doing* with taking the life of a living creature. Although the discussions point to many of the realities of violence in urban life, the responses indicate a resistance to accepting the gratuitous violence that often pervades urban America. Relying on the Community position enabled the readers to work through and sustain common values evidenced through discussions about moral issues.

Family Position

The third position of Family stands out as probably the easiest to pinpoint. When the students tapped into the familial aspects of their culture, they situated themselves as members of families and assumed certain roles and perspectives from this point of view. Indeed, a monolithic view of family did not surface, but the importance of family stood out. Below the students speak to the book's theme of families and their loyalties and obligations to each other. This discussion took place in response to Byron making charges at the grocery store without his parent's permission.

Jerome: He took what his parents were going to [then have to] pay for.
Cameron: I wouldn't do that because I would get found out. Would your parents say, oh that's fine…?
Jerome: If it was my mom, it would depend on how much it is.

As they interpreted this brief but significant event in the text, the participants did so through the perspective of sons who aimed to understand elements in the storyline such as why the parents might respond to the protagonist in particular ways. In this example, the students' textual interpretations are linked to contemporary views of their parents and the expectations they hold. Because authors cannot include everything in a book, readers insert their own story imaginings as a method of constructing meaning (Iser, 1972).

Peers Position

Finally, the Peers position is also central to this theory, particularly because during middle school the peer group heavily influences youth. The participants in our research often responded to the book in keeping with their adolescent developmental stage and affiliations. The Peers position was shaped by the readers' common interests, memberships and values. These features supported readings that constructed multiple hypotheses and considered varying viewpoints about what was read. Here, the students relied on a previous adolescent peer group outing they shared to explain why Byron enjoyed buying things on credit in the story. The students talked as peers with many common shared experiences as the basis for interpretation. They used adolescent-friendly examples, i.e., spending time at the Fun Factory, (a family arcade) to explain their literary interpretations.

Jerome: First he [Byron] goes and gets cookies because he can get the stuff for free. Like when we went to … Fun Factory yesterday this machine kept giving out all of these basketballs and all of these free turns.
Cameron: I don't see how that was the same thing cause no one is really paying for it.
Isaiah: It's like saying you have unlimited money.

The Peers position allowed the readers to "…position themselves above the dynamics of the narrative: to stand outside and above it, as it were, in order to take on new perspectives in relation to the story" (Sipe, 1996, p. 200). This was evident as the discussion went on to include movies, sports, celebrity boxing and music. Responses expressed values and what Giroux (1993) describes as meanings about relationships with others inside and outside of one's world. The strength of salient textual themes fostered intertextual connections with social activities, movies, sports and music.

Discussion and Conclusion

> The vast question of how culture shapes, constrains, and enables literary response is an area under active investigation....All of these factors make it important to contextualize children's responses to literature and to seek to understand the ways in which a diversity of response from a diversity of cultures can enrich literary discussion and interpretation. (Sipe, 1999, p. 126)

As Sipe suggests above, throughout our scholarly careers we have come to understand literary responses as powerfully personal evocations influenced by both readers and stories. Our reader response theory points to the ways these transactions are often mediated by the space one occupies in the world. The youths' responses to *The Watsons Go to Birmingham* (Curtis, 1995) offer illuminating examples of the types of richly contextualized interpretations readers can have. The significance of derived cultural positions embedded in Homeplace offer important implications for understanding how middle grade youth position themselves in relationship to texts with strong cultural fabric. In the four examples, response functioned in a spiraling or overlapping process in which Ethnic Group, Community, Family and Peers each contributed to a lived through experience that Rosenblatt (1985) describes as an ongoing organic process. In Fig. 1 the positions can be seen as "aspects or phases of a total situation" (p. 98). The figure illuminates positioned knowledge coming from the literature, reader and the real cultural world designated as Homeplace. This graphically depicted theory only represents approximations of the children's meanings. In practical application, the participants' interpretations are not so tidy and easily categorized. Rather, the responses are overlapping, transient and often revised, as is consistent with the nature of cultural practices and the fast-paced give and take of discussions.

In this theory, we aim to encapsulate culture (and its embedded practices) as a four pronged heuristic for the purpose of discussion. Similarly, with respect to the multifaceted concept of reading, the proposed theory addresses just one of many facets of the reading process which includes areas such as: interests and motivations, skills and interpretive strategies, cognitive development, approaches to a text, creativity and imagination, ways of assimilating knowledge and visual processing. We intend not to depict the entire reading process, but rather the ways readers culturally position themselves when engaging with texts. We also demonstrate how various features and passages from a multicultural book call forth certain types of positioned responses. The theory explains why two racially or ethnically similar children might share similar or very different interpretations of a story.

We believe this theory offers scholars and teachers of children's and young adult literature a lens through which to better situate literary interpretations. Understanding that a range of cultural positions factors into students' meaning making compels us, we argue, to mine texts more carefully for cultural milieu as well as find acceptance with a broader range of literary interpretations. Students depend on us to locate, when appropriate, the cultural access points that will enable a story to resonate and become meaningful for them. As such, we are advantaged by both valuing and more deeply understanding a wide variety of culturally positioned responses. The pedagogical possibilities in this area are broadened when we both include many different kinds of multicultural literature and then accept as valid and/or build from responses deriving from far reaching links (e.g., racism) or really nuanced connections (e.g., the Fun Factory arcade) as found within students' lives. Figuring out when and how one position becomes focal while reading and if certain features from African American (or any kind of multicultural) narratives regularly solicit certain positions, are the types of inquiries both scholars and teachers can jointly explore. In the end, through this theory we intend for those working in the literacy field to better understand and think more deeply about, "…how culture, race, [and] ethnicity…both enable and constrain response to literature, and thus shape literary understanding" (Sipe. 2008, p. 241).

References

Beach, R. (1993). *A Teacher's Introduction to Reader-Response Theories.* Urbana, IL: National Council of Teachers of English.
Bishop, R.S. (2007). *Free Within Ourselves: The Development of African American Children's Literature.* Portsmouth, NH: Heinemann.
Bleich, D. (1976). Pedagogical Directions in Subjective Criticism. *College English, 37,* 454–467.
Brooks, W. (2003). Accentuating, Preserving, and Unpacking: Exploring Interpretations of Family Relationships with African-American Adolescents. *Journal of Children's Literature, 29*(2), 78–84.
Brooks, W. (2006). Reading Representations of Themselves: Urban Youth Use Culture and African American Textual Features to Develop Literary Understandings. *Reading Research Quarterly, 41*(4), 372–393.
Browne, S., & Brooks, W. (2008). Historical Fiction and "Cultural Evocations" in a Community Based Literary Club. In W. Brooks, & J. McNair (Eds.), *Embracing, Evaluating and Examining African American Children's and Young Adult Literature* (pp. 97–110). Lanham: Scarecrow Press.
Cai, M. (2002). *Multicultural Literature for Children and Young Adults: Reflections on Critical Issues.* Westport, CT: Greenwood Press.
Curtis, C.P. (1995). *The Watsons Go to Birmingham-1963.* New York: Delacorte Press.
Gates, H. (1989). *Talk that Talk* (pp. 15–19). New York: Simon and Schuster.
Giroux, H. (1993). Literacy and the Politics of Difference. In Colin Lankshear, & Peter McLaren (Eds.), *Critical Literacy: Politics, Praxis, and the Postmodern.* New York: SUNY Press.
Harris, V. (1990). African American Children's Literature: The First One Hundred Years. *Journal of Negro Education, 59,* 540–554.
Harris, V. (1992). Contemporary Griots: African American Writers of Children's Literature. In V. Harris (Ed.), *Teaching Multicultural Literature in Grades k-8.* Norwood, MA: Christopher Gordon.
Hamilton, V. (1967). *Zeely.* New York: Simon & Schuster.
Hooks, B. (1990). *Yearning, Race, Gender, and Cultural Politics.* Boston, MA: South End Press.
Iser, W. (1972). The Reading Process: A Phenomenological Approach. *New Literary History, 3,* 279–299.
Johnson, D. (1990). *Telling Tales: The Pedagogy and Promise of African American Literature for youth.* Westport, CT: Greenwood Press.
Louie, B. (2006). Guiding Principles for Teaching Multicultural Literature. *The Reading Teacher, 59,* 438–448.
McNair, J.C. (2008). A Comparative Analysis of *The Brownies' Book* and Contemporary African American Children's Literature Written by Patricia C. McKissack. In W.M. Brooks, & J.C. McNair (Eds.), *Embracing, Evaluating, and Examining African American Children's and Young Adult Literature* (pp. 3–29). Lanham, MD: Scarecrow Press.
Myers, W. (1988). *Scorpions.* New York, NY: Scholastic.
Rabinowitz, P. (1987). *Before Reading: Narrative Conventions and the Politics of Interpretation.* Columbus: Ohio University Press.

Rosenblatt, L. (1982). The Literary Transaction: Evocation and Response. *Theory Into Practice, 21*, 268–277.

Rosenblatt, L. (1985). Viewpoints: Transaction versus interaction—A terminological rescue operation. *Research in the Teaching of English, 19*, 96–107.

Rountree, W. (2008). *Just us Girls: The Contemporary African American Young Adult Novel*. New York: Peter Lang.

Sims, R. (1982). *Shadow and Substance: Afro-American Experience in Contemporary Children's Fiction*. Urbana, IL: National Council of Teachers of English.

Sipe, L. (1996). *The construction of literary understanding by first and second graders in response to picture storybook readalouds*. Dissertation. Retrieved from Proquest Database on January 13, 2012. http://libproxy.temple.edu/login?url=http://proquest.umi.com.libproxy.temple.edu/pqdweb?did=739489911&sid=3&Fmt=2&clientId=8673&RQT=309&VName=PQD. Document ID: 739489911

Sipe, L. (1999). Children's Response to Literature: Author, Text, Reader, Context. *Theory Into Practice, 38*, 120–129.

Sipe, L. (2008). *Storytime: Young Children's Literary Understanding in the Classroom*. New York: Teacher's College Press.

Smith, K.P. (Ed.). (2001). *African-American Voices in Young Adult Literature: Tradition, Transition, Transformation*. Metuchen, NJ: Scarecrow Press.

Strauss, A., & Corbin, J. (1998). Grounded Theory Methodology: An Overview. In N. Denzin, & Y. Lincoln (Eds.), *Strategies of Qualitative Inquiry*. Thousand Oaks, CA: SAGE.

Taylor, M. (1987). *The Friendship*. New York: Dial Books.

Tompkins, J. (Ed.). (1980). *Reader-Response from Formalism to Post-Structuralism*. Baltimore, MD: Johns Hopkins University Press.

Walach, S. (2008). Speaking My Mind: So far from the Bamboo Grove: Multiculturalism, Historical Context, and Close Reading. *English Journal., 97*(3), 16–22.

COMMEMORATIVE ISSUE FOR DR. LAWRENCE SIPE

A Tribute to Dr. Sipe's Memory: Recounting His Final Lessons Teaching Young Adult Fiction, Spring 2011

Emily Sokol

Published online: 15 February 2012
© Springer Science+Business Media, LLC 2012

EDUC 666: Young Adult Fiction—May 2011

I had the privilege and the pleasure of taking *Literature for Children and Adolescents* with Dr. Sipe in the Fall 2010. The following semester, I enrolled in Dr. Sipe's *Education 666: Young Adult Fiction*. It would be his final course, one he would not teach to the end. Still his impact on me is profound; his impression is ever lasting.

When I set out to take Dr. Sipe's Young Adult Fiction course, I thought YAF was just another genre of literature I should study. I imagined the language would be simplified, the subjects would be adolescent, and the content would be juvenile. For these reasons and in spite of them too, I believed reading and discussing YAF might fuel my ability to design engaging curriculum. I speculated it might compel me to connect with students by allowing us to share a common knowledge and familiarity of texts. In hindsight, I was only partially correct. Mostly, however, I misunderstood the utility and value that the form (not genre) of YAF offers in promoting learning, development, and response.

At the end of this course, I came to realize YAF is less about "what is," and more about what it offers. I learned to value YAF as more than a mere list of authors and titles to stock on bookshelves and suggest to students. Instead YAF "holds potential in focusing analysis on aspects of literacy beyond the purely cognitive and academic" (Wissman, 2008, p. 152). The books and the subjects taken up inside them prompt us to enter what might otherwise be uncomfortable but critical

---

Emily Sokol enrolled in the Reading, Writing, Literacy Master's program at the University of Pennsylvania in the Fall of 2010. She took *Literature for Children & Adolescents* with Dr. Sipe in the Fall and *Young Adult Fiction* with Dr. Sipe in the Spring. She graduated with a M.S.ED in July, 2011.

E. Sokol (✉)
Master of Science in Education, Language and Literacy in Education Division, Graduate School of Education, University of Pennsylvania, 3700 Walnut Street, Philadelphia, PA 19104-6216, USA
e-mail: emily.sokol@gmail.com

conversations, providing the space to talk in manageable and safe ways. Margaret Finders says it well when she argues,

> While many teachers may admit that establishing a safe haven is elusive, it is most often held up as a noble goal. I would argue that such a goal is both impossible and undesirable. Such a goal renders the political charge surrounding a classroom neutral. It denies disparate positions of power in the classroom and in the larger culture (Finders, 1997, p. 118).

Where young adults are sometimes reluctant and/or embarrassed to talk to adults about peer pressure, relationships, substance abuse, depression, and/or the challenges and joys of growing up, thinking these topics are too "uncomfortable," YAF provides an opportunity for adolescents and adults, students and teachers, children and parents, to take up the dialogue "comfortably." In effect, through personal experience and observation, I maintain YAF is not just a form of literature; it is a tool for entering discomfort "comfortably." When "tough talk" surfaced in our classroom this past Spring, critical inquiry and critical conversation often ensued.

Dr. Sipe urged his students to not oversimplify. His course called on voices of immigrants, criminals, pubescent teenagers, jocks, and atheists, to name a few. We also explored how vast YAF's readership might be: "preteens looking ahead, true teens excited to see their own experiences in print, young adults eager to leave childhood and its literature behind," and adults connecting to a time and place that either once was or still is (Aronson, 1998, p. 1). Having the opportunity to watch and listen to Dr. Sipe read a picture book to a class or discuss a plotline with his students, one could see how much he honored all ages and stories. Refusing to generalize adolescents or adolescence, he asked tough questions and led thoughtful conversations. I think one of Dr. Sipe's greatest joys in teaching his *Young Adult Fiction* course came with recognizing this complicated and enriching characteristic that defined YAF.

I reflect on three lessons I learned throughout the course; each supports the notion that YAF provides an entry to take up uncomfortable but critical topics.

Lesson #1: Don't be Afraid to Raise the Volume

I felt apprehension while reading Chris Lynch's *Inexcusable* (2005) in tandem with Laurie Halse Anderson's *Speak* (2001), and Pete Hautman's *Godless* (2004) in conjunction with Nancy Garden's *Endgame* (2006). To begin, I feared the dark, dangerous, and criminal might resonate personally with students. I worried students might empathize with Kier, Gigi, Melinda, Eric, Lori, Jason, Shin, or Gray. They might connect as victims, bystanders, or potential persecutors, and that felt wrong to me. How could we read about characters who raped, murdered, ran away from home, abused drugs, defaced public property, shot a gun in school, or committed suicide, without endorsing such behavior in return? However, as we voiced these concerns, and considered the effect of talking about these topics, themes, conflicts, and characters, we knew our fears were misplaced. The books invited "real" into our learning space. In many ways they empowered me to think more objectively about emotional subjects; they gave me insight into varied perspectives and possibilities. We learned to be critical readers, consumers, students, and educators because of the trust our professor placed in us. I determined I would expect no less from my students, from other young adults.

Dr. Sipe's decision to divide the class with Lynch's *Inexcusable* and Anderson's *Speak* made for a powerful lesson on the politics of rape, gender, and the silence that occurs across each. His choice to juxtapose the narrative voices—one victim, one criminal—each recounted through the perspective of an adolescent, made for a thoughtful analysis and conversation about narrative power. Had we only read from one perspective, our understanding of rape or crime might have been reduced. In truth, his pedagogical decision helped us to explore guilt on a deeper level. How appropriate that one of our earliest readings for the course literally took up the cause to bring silences to the surface.

We were introduced to the concept of "abjection" the week we read Hautman's *Godless* (2004) and Garden's *Endgame* (2006). Many weeks we had a choice between two titles and half the class would read each. Thematically linked, the pairings were a way that Dr. Sipe exposed us to more titles and connections. As individuals we did not necessarily read two books a week, but we left knowing about both, thinking about the ways they overlapped, compared, and complemented each other. I realized, sometimes simply being present in a classroom when critical inquiry and tough talk occurs can be sufficient to stimulate empathy. Dr. Sipe didn't shy away from tough topics in his syllabus; for that I am grateful.

Lesson #2: Sharing Equates to Caring

Dr. Sipe introduced us to a number of characters and plot lines that were driven by love and/or infatuation. In each case, we could discuss the thrill and angst of love, sexuality, and romance through a vehicle of the "hypothetical;" he modeled how to promote a safe and relevant classroom.

We explored Rachel Cohn and David Levithan's *Nick & Norah's Infinite Playlist* (2006), Louise Rennison's *Angus Thongs, and Full Frontal Snogging* (1999), and Alex Sanchez's *Rainbow Boys* (2001). Offering a variety of "coming-of-age" novels, Dr. Sipe also provided a sampling of assorted love stories: Nick and Norah exemplified a love divided by class; Georgia and Aaron (a.k.a. sex god) typified high school love across grade level (Georgia is a freshman/minor, Aaron a senior); Jason, Kyle, and Nelson represented a love between boys.

Our study of Sanchez' *Rainbow Boys* was arguably my favorite class of the semester, as Dr. Sipe planned a lesson that wove theory, interview, YAF, research, and personal conversation. I can recall entering the class feeling fond of Jason, Kyle, and Nelson, the three main characters from Sanchez's novel, and defensive towards Crisp, a scholar critiquing these boys. Recalling some of our earlier questions about YAF, I was offended by Crisp's assertion that "The trouble with Rainbow Boys" (2009) was it "reinforce[d] heterosexual stereotype of what gay kids are like" (Sipe, 2008, p. 266). I disagreed with his point. Nevertheless, the intersection of Crisp's critique besides Dr. Sipe's interview of Sanchez, in complement with my own thoughts and reactions to the fictional boys, made for a fascinating and invaluable learning moment. I found my opinions softened and my perspective broadened by all the voices Dr. Sipe invited to speak that day.

Just as characters were rounded and complicated through conversation, so too, I found, were Dr. Sipe and Alex Sanchez; having a transcript and window to their private conversation alongside others' reactions, made them all the more real and human too. It became the impetus for personal information to be disclosed and trust to be formed. When Dr. Sipe read excerpts from his interview with Sanchez to the class, the distinction between fiction and truth disintegrated, the division between professor and student ceased. So, on one level the YAF made us challenge, critique, and question hegemonic normative binaries related to gender and sexuality, binaries we perhaps never realized we believed or performed. On the other hand, Dr. Sipe's participation and facilitation of those conversations allowed intimacy and community to build. The book, in this case, helped me find new ways for connecting and relating to adults—my professor, my peers, and the author. The experience helped me realize how important it is to provide students rich, relatable examples of life as it truly unfolds (Quinn, 2001, p. 58). The lesson helped me appreciate a teacher's courage. When Dr. Sipe shared personal information with his students that afternoon he raised the volume and showed he cared.

Lesson #3: Model Greatness, Expect Greatness, Inspire Greatness

Sanchez says, "what makes YA books so exciting nowadays … is that these are issues that all of us in modern society grapple with and try to reconcile in our lives" (Sipe, 2008, p. 268). Many texts this semester took up this call: An Na's *A Step From Heaven* (2001), Yang's *American Born Chinese* (2006), Green's *Looking for Alaska* (2005), Anderson's *Feed* (2002), and Myer's *Fallen Angels* (1988).

Young Ju in *A Step From Heaven* and Jin Wang, Danny, Chin-Kee, and the Monkey King in *American Born Chinese* narrate their struggles and hardships of immigration and coming-of-age. Sometimes, the cultural clashes they face are devastating. I was troubled by Young Ju's family dynamics, bothered by Yang's caaricatures, made uncomfortable by the development of certain characters. And yet, as I speculated with Rennison's intent, I suspected that this discomfort had purpose.

In many ways, this process of inquiry was mirrored explicitly in Green's *Looking for Alaska*. The book is written in a countdown of the "Before" and "After" of Miles' experience with the "Great Perhaps;" readers mourn Alaska's death (accident or suicide?) and Miles' regret in life. Coupled with grief and resolve to take blame and seek forgiveness, this story was hard to read and gripping all the same. Though ultimately hopeful, it showed that "great" does not exist without its fair share of tragic. It was timely that Dr. Sipe assigned this text in the same week he passed away; the subject of untimely death was certainly real.

On a lighter note, Anderson's *Feed* explored the notion of choice and chance through a dystopian, science-fiction tale of adventures between the moon, Earth, and futuristic world of in-between. It was a text that Dr. Sipe loved to talk about and recommend; I can still hear him reading the first page grinning amusingly: "Link Arwaker was like, 'I'm so null,' and Marty was all, 'I'm null too, unit,' but I mean we were all pretty null" asking the class, "isn't this great!" (Anderson, 2002, p. 3) In this futuristic time and place, where nature is synthetic, communities live in "clouds," cars fly, people travel to outer space, weather is controlled by man-made gadgets, scientists clone people in place of birth, trend-setters sport lesions when toxicity becomes too tough to fight, conversations take place without the utterance of a verbal, brains connect to the internet through surgical feeds, and people download memories to share thoughts, Anderson has his reader question whether society has advanced or regressed. Even more to the point, he has us wonder, "How far off is our reality from this fictitious one?" Readers might question, "What influences my "choices" in my world?" Teachers might ask students to ponder similar queries too, and in the guise of fictitious hardship, we begin to build dialogue and inquiry about our own lives.

The last text of the semester, Myers' *Fallen Angels* (1988), illustrated this point perfectly. Inspired by his brother's death, Myers chose to set his tale in the Vietnam War. Driving this story is the "the major issue... and the one Perry wrestles with repeatedly ... 'Why are we here?'" (Bishop, 1991, p. 91). Instead of criminalizing one side against the other, Myers maintains a focus for human complexity, a reality that no matter if people are in wartime or peacetime, good and evil are not binary. His story also begs attention to race, class, power, and identity. Perhaps most discomforting, it leaves readers wondering how its subject applies to present-day.

Ultimately, these texts ask readers to inquire. By posing tough questions, inviting the challenge, prompting discomfort, Dr. Sipe showed us how to reconsider YAF, pedagogy, and practice. He inspired us to raise the bar of expectation for our students, our world, and ourselves, and he showed us how literature might be one of the greatest vehicles to effect change.

Summative Thoughts

While the course readings have prompted many studies into what the coming-of-age might entail, I continue to believe we cannot "buy into the 'myth of universal adolescence'" (Finders, 1997, p. 123). Such a treatment "reduc[es] possibilities for disrupting the status quo" (Finders, 1997, p. 123); it values *safety* and *comfort* over relevance, truth, and function. In ways, "it is much like adolescent life, filled with transitions, confusions, and overlappings of adult and childhood sensibilities" (Aronson, 1998, p. 4). With this understanding, we cannot treat YAF as simply "problem novels;" they are tools and entry points for young adults to engage with real situations, real concerns, real emotions. More than that, they are the bridge between young adults and adults, adolescence and the coming-of-age. Dr. Sipe embodied this belief in the ways he engaged with each of these texts and in the ways he loved children's books, his work, and his students.

On a personal level, the semester's texts brought me closer to my classmates and my professors. After Dr. Sipe's passing they were my link for remembering and honoring his passion for YAF, literacy, and storytelling; these books and the memory of Dr. Sipe's charisma, passion, wisdom, and joy were the bonds for connecting me to my classmates and Susan Lea, the teacher who followed Dr. Sipe. Together we gained appreciation for the very human element in reading, conversing, and teaching. We learned YAF makes it possible, meaningful, and more comfortable to take up critical conversation. It connects readers to people and it makes reading and literacy applicable along the way.

In an effort to build criticality, confidence, and awareness, we should think about YAF with a broader appreciation. It's too easy to dismiss YAF because its name is misleading. To do so would result in a missed opportunity; I feel fortunate I did not miss mine. I can confidently say the work I started this semester is only the beginning of a lifetime of appreciation that comes from reading, teaching, learning and advocating YAF. Thank you Dr. Sipe.

Afterward

Every time I go to the bookstore now I leave a little time to peruse the Young Adult Fiction section. I have an ongoing list of recommendations. When I consider why I read these books, I can answer with many reasons—to connect and recommend titles to students, to escape into other worlds, to seek adventures, counsel, and amusement. Mostly, though, Dr. Sipe's teaching, in tandem with other fantastic professors at the University of Pennsylvania's Graduate School of Education, has taught me to be inquisitive. The books are an avenue for conversation, communication, and connection, and they are windows into other's minds, belief systems, and concerns. They are springboards and catalysts for identity, discovery, progress, and community, but they are incomplete, missed opportunities if we neglect talking about them, deconstructing them, analyzing, responding, and considering their application to our world(s).

Dr. Sipe was a great professor because he embodied what he believed. He loved his students; he loved the power of the story; he loved finding complexity in unexpected places. He will forever be a mentor for me because he taught me through words and action; he led me by model and instruction. He courageously confronted the dark stuff, shared the personal stuff, and questioned the tough stuff alongside his students in body and spirit this past Spring 2011. He modeled greatness, expected greatness, inspired greatness; he inspired me.

References

Anderson, M.T. (2002). *Feed*. Somerville, MA: Candlewick Press.
Anderson, Laurie Halse. (2001). *Speak* New York, NY: Penguin Group.
Aronson, Marc. (1998). *YA talk: The challenge and the glory of young adult literature. Booklist: Youth – YA talk – Thinking about CD-ROMs*. http://www.ala.org.booklist/v93/55yat4.html.
Bishop, Rudene Sims. (1991). *Presenting Dean Myers*. Chapter 5: *Of Battles and Brotherhood: Myers the War Novelist*. Boston, MA: Twayne Publishing.

Cohn, Rachel, & Levithan, David. (2006). *Nick and Norah's Infinite Playlist*. New York: Random House.
Crisp, Thomas. (2009). The Trouble with Rainbow Boys. *Children's Literature in Education, 29*, 237–261.
Finders, M. (1997). *Just Girls: Hidden Literacies and Life in Junior High*. New York: Teachers College Press.
Garden, (2006). *Endgame*. Orlando, FL: Harcourt Inc.
Green, John. (2005). *Looking for Alaska*. New York: Penguin House.
Hautman, Pete. (2004). *Godless*. New York: Simon & Schuster Books for Young Readers.
Lynch, Chris. (2005). *Inexcusable*. New York: Simon Pulse.
Myers, Walter Dean. (1988). *Fallen Angels*. New York: Scholastic Inc.
Na, An. (2001). *A Step from Heaven*. New York: Penguin Group.
Quinn, Elaine J. (2001). Between Voice and Voicelessness: Transacting Silence in Laurie Halse Anderson's *Speak*. *The Alan Review, 29*(1), 54–58.
Rennison, Louise. (1999). *Angus, Thongs and Full-Frontal Snogging: Confessions of Georgia Nicolson*. London: Harper Tempest.
Sanchez, Alex. (2003). *Rainbow Boys*. New York: Simon Pulse.
Sipe, Lawrence. (2008). A Conversation with Alex Sanchez and Lawrence Sipe. *Children's Literature in Education, 39*, 263–268.
Wissman, Kelly. (2008). "Spinning Themselves into Poetry": Images of Urban Adolescent Writers in Two Novels for Young Adults. *Children's Literature in Education, 40*, 149–167.
Yang, Gene Luen. (2006). *American Born Chinese*. New York: Square Fish.

COMMEMORATIVE ISSUE FOR DR. LAWRENCE SIPE

Reading Picturebooks *as Literature*: Four-to-Six-Year-Old Children and the Development of Literary Competence

Coosje van der Pol

Published online: 15 February 2012
© The Author(s) 2012. This article is published with open access at Springerlink.com

Abstract This article explores what it means to be a competent reader of picture storybooks by examining the abilities of some 4–6-year-olds, who were read stories aloud in class. Jonathan Culler's concept of "literary competence" was used to tease out the children's implicit knowledge of the structures and conventions that enable them to read a work of fiction as literature. From a more practical point of view, Lawrence Sipe's class-based work, discussing picture storybooks with first and second grade children, provided some useful guidelines. This current study draws on an educational design experiment involving "literary conversation guides," which help probe children's understanding of such story features as character and irony.

Keywords Literary competence · Pre-school children · Picturebooks · Educational design experiment

Introduction

In the lower grades of Dutch primary schools picture storybooks are read aloud to children almost every day. An important objective of reading aloud is to promote literacy development and vocabulary learning in particular (see, among others,

---

Coosje van der Pol has a Master's in Culture Studies from Tilburg University and a PhD in Culture Studies from the same university. She is currently working as a lecturer on the "Children's Literature" Master's course at Tilburg University and also lectures on "Sociology of the Arts" at the same university. She writes picturebook reviews and articles on children's responses to picturebooks for various journals (e.g. *De Leeswelp*, *Leesgoed*) and also gives guest lectures at teacher training colleges in the Netherlands and Flanders.

C. van der Pol (✉)
Department of Language and Culture Studies, Faculty of Humanities, Tilburg University, Dante Building, Room 222, P.O. Box 90153, 5000 LE Tilburg, The Netherlands
e-mail: j.a.vdrpol@uvt.nl

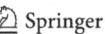

Bus et al., 1995). Also picturebook read-alouds serve as "stepping-stones" for various educational and pedagogical activities, for instance understanding traffic signs or learning how to fly a kite (Van der Pol, 2010). These kinds of reading take an instrumental approach to picture storybooks and are usually less concerned with literary skills or "literary competence." One might wonder why the most obvious thing that can be done with children's literature, that is to read it *as literature*, does not receive more attention in primary education.

Although literary competence has become more of an issue in primary education over the last few years there is no consensus on what the concept actually involves. Also there is very little practical knowledge on the use of the concept with young children (Van der Pol, 2010). When it is mentioned in professional publications or in policy documents literary competence often appears to be used as a catch-all term (including activities such as searching for books in the library) or is described in a very general sense (for instance, as "the ability to read literary texts").

In the learning objectives of the first two years of primary education (in the Netherlands called groups 1 and 2, for pupils aged four to six) literary competence is not mentioned as such. Although it could be said to be involved in the intermediate objectives of Dutch language-learning (Verhoeven et al., 1999), more specifically in the topics of "book orientation" (concerned with issues like title, writer, illustrator, text, pictures and pages) and "narrative understanding" (concerned with issues like characters, episodes and setting). Teachers, however, often find it difficult to address the abstract issues involved in "narrative understanding" with young children. It is therefore relevant to find out how picturebook read-alouds can stimulate the development of narrative understanding or literary competence, understood as knowledge of the ways in which stories are structured and create meaning. For this reason, a PhD research project[1] was carried out that investigates what signs of literary competence 4–6-year-olds already display and how that competence can be expanded by reading picture storybooks and talking about them in a literature-orientated way.

Literary Understanding and Literary Competence

In his award-winning study "The Construction of Literary Understanding by First and Second Graders in Oral Response to Picture Storybook Read-Alouds," Lawrence Sipe (2000) focussed on the social construction of literary understanding indicated by children's verbal responses to picture storybooks. Sipe looked at the literary understanding of 6- and 7-year-olds through multiple theoretical lenses, such as semiotics, visual aesthetic theory, schema and cognitive flexibility theory, and a range of theories from contemporary literary criticism. The concept of

---

[1] The PhD project was part of a larger project called "Picture books and concept development" (PiCo), a multi-centre project in the Netherlands involving, in addition to "literary competence," the concepts of social and emotional development, and mathematics. Each concept was developed empirically using educational design experiments (Cobb et al., 2003) and subsequently tested in a randomised controlled trial. The literary competence project has been published in a PhD thesis in Dutch with a summary in English (Van der Pol, 2010).

"literary competence" was also included in Sipe's theoretical lenses. He referred to it rather briefly by saying that:

> Children and (their teacher) together construct their own implicit definition of literary competence (Culler, 1975) within the constraints and opportunities of their interpretative community (Fish, 1980). (Sipe, 2000, p. 260)

Culler's concept of literary competence, which is rooted in structuralism, Sipe considered a "traditional perspective" (Sipe, 2000, p. 255) on literary understanding. From the structuralist point of view, Sipe continued:

> stories may be viewed as stimulating the perception of formal patterns (e.g., the home-away-home pattern represented in *Where the Wild Things Are* [Sendak, 1963], or binary opposites like good/evil or beauty/ugliness), which are useful for understanding how the story works. (Sipe, 2000, p. 255)

Literary understanding, Sipe argued, may, however, be conceptualised in a broader, richer, and more textured way by applying concepts from a range of theories that are integrated by the idea of literary understanding as a social construction. In his study Sipe modelled children's responses to picture storybooks into five conceptual categories of literary understanding: the analytical, the intertextual, the personal, the transparent and the performative, each category being characterised by different stances, actions, and functions. Analytical responses, in which children deal with a picturebook as an object or cultural product, represent 73 per cent of all the children's spontaneous responses. When responding analytically, children stay with the story and make comments that reflect an analytical stance, for instance about the book as a cultural artefact (produced by an author, illustrator, publisher and printer), about the language in which the story is told, the illustrations, narrative interpretations and the relation between fiction and reality. According to Sipe these five categories constitute the enactments of three basic literary impulses: the hermeneutic impulse (the drive to understand the story and interpret it), the personalising impulse (to link the story to the self and the personal experience), and the aesthetic impulse (either responding receptively to the story as a lived-through experience or using the story as the platform for one's own creative expression). Sipe derives from this the idea that "Literary understanding is the dynamic process whereby these three impulses are activated and synergistically interact with each other" (Sipe, 2000, p. 271).

In his study Sipe raised some interesting ideas about Culler's concept of literary competence. But since Sipe was particularly interested in a *multifaceted* conception of literary understanding, he did not explore the idea of literary competence in great detail. We therefore are not sure what the suggested implicit definition of literary competence by children and their teacher involves; and whether it can be made explicit when we wish to describe it. Also it is unclear what constitutes the possible constraints and opportunities of an interpretative community of 4–6-year-olds. And can the opportunities be expanded by offering teachers and children tools for a more conscious *literary* approach to children's books? When taking a closer look at Culler's concept of literary competence, it proves to have a strong educational potential which so far has not received any in-depth exploration as far as young children are concerned.

Literary Competence

Culler (2002/1975) has based his idea of literary competence on an analogy with Noam Chomsky's (1965) concept of linguistic competence. Chomsky argues that to understand a sequence of words *as a sentence* one must be familiar with the system—or structure—of the language in which the sentence is spoken. People, even at a very young age, have an internalised grammar which Chomsky calls "linguistic competence." Without this competence a sentence (or rather a sequence of sounds) will be meaningless to the listener, literally "nothing but hot air." By analogy, Culler suggests we may think of structure and meaning as properties of literary works. A literary work has meaning only when it is read, or listened to, in a particular way; when it is read "as literature" (Culler, 2002, p. 149). Literature, Culler argues, therefore depends on particular modes of reading. To read a text *as literature*:

> is not to make one's mind a *tabula rasa* and approach it without preconceptions; one must bring to it an implicit understanding of the operations of literary discourse which tells one what to look for. (ibid, p. 132)

According to Culler the notion of literary competence does not presume, however, that there is just one proper (competent) way to read literature. If in an interpretative community the practices of reading literature are that readers may interpret works in a variety of ways, then that is a fact about literary competence. The only presumption the concept of literary competence entails, Culler argues, is

> that there is learning involved, in coming to read literature, as in learning a language—that readers do acquire both sets of categories and procedures for their application, so that there is something—call it "competence"—to be described. (ibid, p. xi)

Literary competence therefore is both a characteristic of readers (an internalised story grammar) and a description of that competence (a descriptive grammar or poetics). Culler's theoretical discourse on literary competence, however, neither deals with young readers, nor does it go into any possible educational implications. For that reason these issues have been addressed in an educational design experiment.

Educational Design Experiment

Educational design experiments aim at engineering particular forms of learning and systematically studying those forms of learning within a particular context and using particular means (Cobb et al., 2003). During an educational design experiment teachers and researchers work closely together in the classroom. This collaboration allows the development of theories about the children's learning of key concepts within a well defined domain; for example, within literature this might be to appreciate what a "main character" is. Based on patterns in children's reasoning a theory of this type offers insights into the learning process. It also sheds light on the means that encourage that learning; in this case the picture storybooks that are read aloud in the classroom using "literary conversation guides."

Literary conversation guides have been designed to trigger children's thinking about how stories work. This is done by looking at some of the conventions picturebooks employ, for instance showing a picture taken from the story on the front cover. A literary conversation guide also addresses how a particular story is structured and how that structure produces effects such as suspense. There is, for instance, the issue of the intentional distribution of information between reader and character(s) whereby one party is better informed about what will happen in the story than the other. This structural device may lead to suspense or (when the reader knows more) to a sense of superiority in the reader who already knows the protagonist's fate. Each conversation guide contains a brief theoretical description (similar to the above) of a literary phenomenon. It also contains questions and points of attention teachers could use to discuss the phenomenon with children when reading the story. In *Dear Little Lamb*, (Dutch title: *Lief lammetje*,) (Kempter and Weldin, 2006) for instance, a nameless lamb receives letters from a mysterious friend signed with the name Wolfgang. Immediately after looking at the front cover, which shows a wolf with a typewriter, the reader knows the sender's identity. After the second letter the children were asked: "Does Little Lamb actually know who this friend is?" The children established that the characters had not actually met each other yet and that Little Lamb could not see the book cover. The children concluded from this that Little Lamb therefore did not know that Wolfgang is a wolf. They also realised the effect of this: "It is scary because the little lamb has not seen the wolf yet but we have!" a girl commented.

The literary conversation guides were tested and optimised in two classrooms of the same primary school. As in Sipe's (2000) study, the teachers were encouraged to use an open, conversational approach and to try to avoid direct questioning. Each reading-aloud session was videotaped and transcribed. The analyses of children's comments, questions and reasoning offer information on what constitutes the literary competence (as far as the selected topics are concerned) of the participating 4–6-year-olds. In addition to this the observation of classroom interactions provided information about the constraints and opportunities for the children's interpretative community.

Story Characters

The exploration of "story characters" provides a good starting point when reading picturebooks *as literature* because characters are relatively accessible to young readers. Readers tend to identify with characters more than with any other story element (e.g. Applebee, 1978) and story characters can invite readers to become involved in the story. Therefore topics related to characters that are both relevant to the development of literary competence and of interest to young children were identified first. Subsequently picturebooks containing interesting literary conventions or techniques related to story characters were selected and read aloud to children by their own teacher using the literary conversation guides.

Reflection on story characters may start from the idea that in a story one or more figures participate. Also relevant is the notion that story characters are not "real" but entirely depend on literary conventions and cultural codes. Furthermore, literary competent readers can distinguish the main character(s) from the additional characters. By doing so a reader decides to whom he or she should pay most attention and places others in relation to that character, which is an important structuring activity (Culler, 2002).

When asked who participated in a story that had just been read to them, children usually managed to sum up all or most of the characters. Although this may seem like a mere memory-test, the question also encourages children to think of the concept of "character." Interestingly enough, when summing up story characters some children also included non-characters, like the rocks or clouds they had seen in the pictures. This led to classroom discussions about what or who can be story characters and what/who cannot. During these conversations children established that some stories feature inanimate objects as story characters (e.g. the house in Virginia Lee Burton's *The Little House*, 1978/1942) while in other stories houses—and also things like rocks and clouds—are just part of the setting. Such conversations made the children more aware of the literary conventions of character construction.

Obviously, when discussing issues concerning story structure and conventions, this should be done in a vocabulary that is accessible to children. "Who takes part in the story?" or "Who plays a part in the story?" proved to be productive formulations. It is also useful of course to listen to the children's own usage, or in Chomsky's (1965) terms "performance," when discussing literary issues. A 4-year-old boy for instance, described a story character as someone who "walks around in the book." Sometimes children are familiar with a particular literary concept but do not know the corresponding vocabulary yet. In other instances children may not know the concept either. Both situations can be considered "teachable moments" in which the teacher can introduce the literary concept and possibly also the words that refer to it (Langer, 1991). In this educational design experiment, however, teaching terminology like "story characters" was not an issue and the children stayed with descriptions like "the animals who play (or take part) in the story."

Main Characters

Having established who participates in the story, most children managed to identify the main character of that story. Children who successfully pointed out the main character and also managed to explain why he or she is the protagonist answered, for example: "His picture is on the front of the book," "His name is (in) the title of the book," "We see him on every page," or "He's the one who has all the strange adventures." Yet other children clearly related the main character to the role of the hero of the story by saying: "He does everything well," or "He saved his life"; one child even said "He is like the hero." Some children identified the main character correctly but could, however, not explain *why* that character was the most important figure in the story. This suggests that the correct identification of the protagonist may have been done intuitively, in a way that is still pre-reflective. Again, these cases present teachable moments in which knowledge of the subject was "constructed" by children and their teacher in classroom discussions.

Also of interest are responses in which children sum up story characters by relating them (implicitly) to the protagonist, for instance by saying "His mother, his grandmother, his brothers and sisters." Strikingly, these children did not include in their answers the character referred to by the possessive pronoun. It therefore seems that they somehow realise that there is a main character to whom all the others are related, but for some reason they do not mention it. What is more, when asked who the most important character in the story was, these children did not know. This underlines the idea that identifying the main character is sometimes done intuitively and that reflection on the issue may lead to confusion, but at the same time it offers an opportunity to learn about literary conventions.

The literary conversation guides contain various clues to help children to identify the main character. A clue is, for example, that in the illustrations the main character is usually depicted as larger than less important characters. Also the protagonist usually has a personal name, while additional characters often only have generic names (e.g. "the people from the village"). In one illustration from *We Honestly Can Look After Your Dog* (Child, 2005), for example, we see some boys playing football in the background and then they seem to have disappeared from the story completely. A girl described their role as minor figures thus: "Those boys were only there to play some football and went straight back home again."

Informative "Mistakes"

The "mistakes" children make (in their performance) are a useful source of information if one is trying to discern the pupils' underlying literary competence. Also "mistakes" can offer learning opportunities. When asked who is the most important figure in *Cottonwool Colin* (Dutch title: *Watje Wimpie*) (Willis and Ross, 2007) (Figs. 1 and 2) most children correctly identified Colin (a mouse) as the protagonist. But when asked how one can tell that Colin is indeed the most important character, some children answered "Because he is tiny." or "Because his mother took very good care of him." Both these statements are true in this particular story, but these are not *literary* reasons why Colin is the protagonist. In real life, children may find that parents take good care of their little ones, because they find their children important. Other children said that the mother mouse was the most important story character "Because she is the boss," or "Because my mummy and daddy are also important." Still other children said the mad fox in the story was the main character "Because he has sharp teeth." His dangerous jaws definitely make the fox an important character to watch, but they do not make him the story's protagonist. The fox only plays a supporting role in the story, which may be discussed in terms of "he only appears once," "he has no name," or "he does not do much" and so on.

However different they are, these examples of children identifying what is actually a supporting character as the main character, all demonstrate that there are important differences between how things work in the real world and in stories. The two "systems" require different sets of rules and conventions. Whatever makes a

Ze pakt Wimpie in.

tot alleen zijn voeten nog uitsteken.
Nu is hij Watje Wimpie.

Fig. 1 "His mother, his grandmother, his brothers and sisters." Reprinted with permission from De Vries-Brouwers (the publisher): Jeanne Willis and Tony Ross. *Watje Wimpie*. Antwerpen: De Vries-Brouwers, 2007

person important in real life may not apply to the world of the story and vice versa: something a competent reader of literature is aware of.

(Un)Usual Suspects

As Sipe (2000, p. 255) also pointed out, binary opposites are an important concept in structuralist literary theory (going back to Ferdinand de Saussure's claim that in linguistics difference is the most important criterion for creating meaning). Many stories feature pairs like villain/hero, cat/mouse or wolf/sheep. These opposites are important structuring principles for storytelling, which is something that children are often aware of, even if only subconsciously. When a villain enters the scene, for instance, they comment that the hero will be there soon, or when the front cover of the book shows a picture of a wolf they predict that there will be a sheep or a goat in the story too. This confirms that 4–6-year-olds already have some mental schemata about how stories work. Once this is established children can move on to story conventions that are a little more demanding; for instance, the convention that a

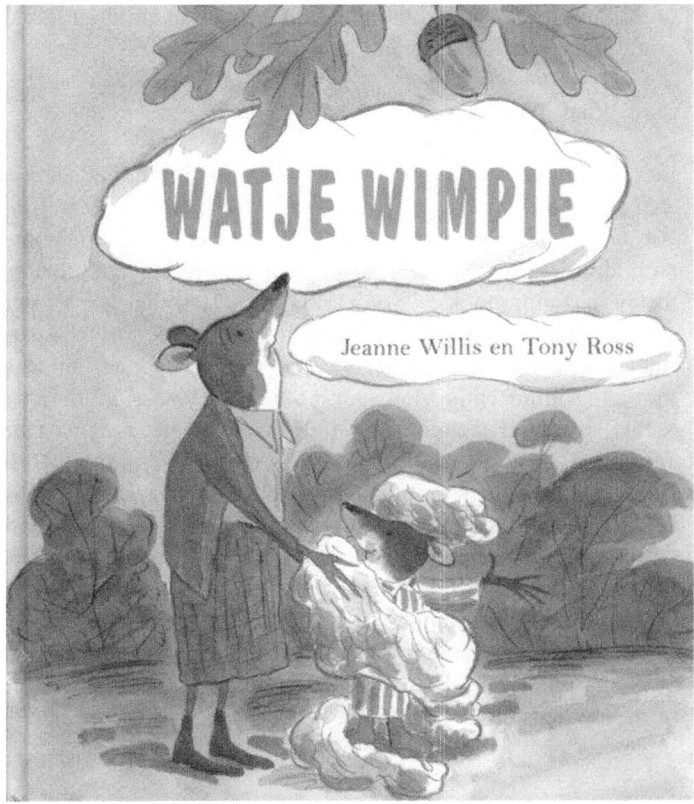

Fig. 2 "His picture is on the front of the book." Reprinted with permission from De Vries-Brouwers (the publisher): Jeanne Willis and Tony Ross. *Watje Wimpie*. Antwerpen: De Vries-Brouwers, 2007

character has some symbolic meaning. The children who participated in the educational design experiment were remarkably familiar with character conventions such as the brave lion, the sly fox or the trusting little lamb. When one of these characters appeared, children usually knew exactly what to expect. In discussing the typical traits of those characters pupils frequently referred to similar figures in other stories. Their comments often included references to stories from popular culture, ranging from Disney DVDs to stories from the fairytale forest of a well known Dutch theme park, "De Efteling." A lion, for instance, was immediately described as "brave," "strong" and "king of the animals," "like in the Lion King," a 5-year-old boy added.

Once children are familiar with some basic conventions regarding story characters, they will also notice when authors or illustrators play with conventional character traits, for instance by exaggerating or reversing them. This is the case when characters are portrayed ironically: the lion is humble, the fox gets tricked or a wolf and a sheep turn out to be best friends. Children usually realise there is something odd about those characters. A typical reaction—registered when reading *Wolves* (Gravett, 2005) in which, in an "alternative ending," the wolf does not eat the rabbit after all, but has toast with jam instead—was that children found it "funny that a wolf could be a vegetarian."

Irony: "It is not What You Expect"

Using the literary conversation guides the teachers in the educational design experiment helped their pupils to grasp ironic characterisations by using the definition borrowed from Jon Stott (1982): "It is not what you expect." Stott designed for children (in his case 8-year-olds) a simple but effective strategy for interpreting irony in picturebooks: "Something in a story that wasn't what you (or the characters) expected" (ibid, p. 159). Irony in children's stories is usually based on the idea that a reader or a character expects "a" to happen but what *actually* happens is "not-a" (Kümmerling-Meibauer, 1999). For young children to recognise and interpret this structural technique is quite a challenge, not least because the irony is often implicit. Stott was the first to admit that his definition ("It is not what you expect") might be a huge simplification of the complex phenomenon of irony. But then the definition has the pragmatism required for educational design experiments: it emphasises a major element of irony, unexpected discrepancy, and, as such, alerts young readers to be on the lookout. So when children perceive an ironic character or situation as humorous, their teacher could grasp this "teachable moment" and explain that sometimes it can be funny when someone, like a vegetarian wolf (or some*thing*, as is the case in an ironic event), is quite different from how we or another character thought he or she (or it) would be.

Constraints and Opportunities for the Interpretative Community

In his brief discussion of literary competence, Sipe (2000) refers to the fact that children are both constrained and enabled by the rules of their interpretive community. An important constraint on reading picturebooks *as literature* appears to be the kind of response that Sipe named the "personalising impulse." Through this impulse children are able to relate the story to their own lives by making "life-to-text" or "text-to-life" connections (Sipe, 2000, p. 270). This personalising impulse is not entirely trouble-free where the concept of literary competence is concerned. In his theoretical discourse on literary competence, Culler describes the impetuous move from text to life as an "unseemly rush from word to world" (Culler, 2002, p. 151). It is "unseemly" because when reading a text *as literature*, the reader, Culler argues, is supposed to stay with the literary system for as long as possible and explore it in accordance with the rules and conventions of that system. This resembles the kind of response that Sipe (2000, p. 264) describes, where the "children stayed within the text conceived as a union of visual and verbal sign systems," which is an important characteristic of analytical responses. By rushing from the story world to one's own world, effects that are made possible by the story structure (for example ironic interpretations) may be "overruled" by interpretations that are wholly personal or idiosyncratic. This may lead to premature foreclosure, a situation in which the reader does not "allow the text to differentiate itself from ordinary language, to grant maximum scope to the play of formal features and of semantic uncertainties" (Culler, 2002, p. 187).

A paradigmatic case in point occurred when the unmistakably ironic story *Jaap Schaap* (Vis, 2000) (Fig. 3), about a wolf who turns out to be a sheep's best friend, was read aloud. A highly pragmatic 6-year-old boy "solved" the ironic situation by suggesting that "maybe the wolf was just a dog." He continued by explaining his own experiences with dogs that get along with sheep very well. Here the real world forecloses the story's ambiguity, thereby leaving little room for ironic play. The teacher's enthusiastic response to what he thought a smart solution, however, confirmed that in this particular interpretative community "premature foreclosure" was not considered problematic.

In Jean Piaget's (1972) influential theory of the stages of cognitive development, concrete thinking and egocentrism are important characteristics of 4–6-year-olds. But the practice of relating stories to children's own lives is also actively encouraged in the lower grades of Dutch primary education. As argued earlier, stories are often read to learn about the world or to talk about children's own experiences. Children are explicitly invited to make text-to-life and life-to-text connections. However, by inviting empiricism and pragmatism into the story world straightaway, one cuts short the literary play. The result is that children may not read the story *as literature* but rather as an "ordinary account" of the world.

The rather impressive number of stories that 4–6-year-olds already seem to be familiar with (Van der Pol, 2010) offers a wealth of opportunity for their interpretative community. The children who participated in the educational design experiment made some interesting intertextual references, with many of their stories

Fig. 3 Reprinted with permission from Lemniscaat (the publisher): Leendert Jan Vis. *Jaap Schaap*. Rotterdam: Lemniscaat, 2000

deriving from popular culture, such as animation films, TV shows and theme parks. These findings are consistent with Sipe's (2000, p. 264), where intertextual responses referring to stories from different media made up ten per cent of the total number of responses.

Knowledge of stories from popular culture can promote thinking about the ways stories work in children's literature. When encountering a difficult structural technique like a "flashback" in a picture storybook, it may be understood by referring to this phenomenon in films. In one class, some children explained to their classmates that when in animated cartoons a picture becomes a little hazy and the colours fade to black and white, for instance, it means that the action takes place in the past. Films and animated cartoons, obviously, also employ structural techniques such as "gaps" and binary opposites. Considering film and picture storybooks as "allies" (Mackey, 1993; Meek, 1996) therefore offers numerous opportunities for reading picturebooks *as literature*.

Conclusions and Discussion

Culler's notion of literary competence has been used in the above educational design experiments to make explicit the implicit readings of young children, showing what informs their responses, interpretations and solutions to particular textual problems. In short, what competence underlies a certain performance. Of course, competence is itself defined by a particular interpretive community and its norms of what is acceptable; moreover, that normative frame of reference may be adjusted to accommodate new readings if they are communally deemed suitable. However, it will also seek to exclude readings that seem wholly personal or idiosyncratic, for the very reason that to be an experienced reader of literature is "after all, to have gained a sense of what can be done with literary works and thus to have assimilated a system which is largely interpersonal" (Culler, 2002, pp. 148–149).

Children as Structuring Readers

As Sipe (2000) aptly argued, from the structuralist perspective literary understanding has often been conceptualised in a somewhat restrictive or passive way by focusing on formal text characteristics. But Culler's concept of literary competence—though fundamentally structuralist—is neither restrictive nor passive. Reading picturebooks *as literature* is not essentially about the teaching of formal text characteristics but aims to describe what a "structuring reader" (Brooks, 1976) does. Structure therefore need not be considered as an objective property of stories: it emerges in structuring *processes* performed by the reader (albeit on a determinate text). The fact remains, however, that some stories contain more challenging response-inviting structures than others. Also it is true that these "structuring processes" sometimes have to be elicited by thought-provoking questions. By considering children's judgments and intuitions about how stories work we can gain evidence about their structuring activities and underlying literary competence.

By purposefully eliciting literary response to picturebooks this study took a different approach from the research done by Sipe (2000), who studied children's *spontaneous* responses to picture storybooks. In Sipe's study the teacher stayed with her normal routine by encouraging children to talk at any point during the story, but maintained an attitude of acceptance rather than direction or evaluation (Sipe, 2000, pp. 261–262). This raises the question of what would happen to children's literary competence if teachers did nothing out of the ordinary and just read the books they were used to in their usual ways. In our research project these questions were answered by means of a randomised controlled trial in which eighteen classrooms participated. Although this experiment is beyond the scope of the present article, the outcome was that the children who were read the twenty-four picturebooks with the literary conversations guides showed a significant increase in literary competence over those in the control groups. This finding confirms the effectiveness of reading picturebooks *as literature* with the aid of literary conversation guides (Van der Pol, 2010).

The Value of the Linguistic Analogy

When investigating what constitutes literary competence at the ages of 4–6, the analogy with linguistic competence is illuminating indeed. Although young children have not yet received any formal grammar instruction, they do know how sentences are structured and how that structure enables particular meanings and rules out others. They can understand spoken sentences, even sentences they have never heard before. Children—and most adults too—are usually oblivious to these capacities. As far as young children are concerned, linguistic competence develops through learning by doing and by informal instruction. It flourishes best when a child grows up in a context that is rich in language, both spoken and written. This idea has become well-established in terms of "emergent literacy" (e.g. Sulzby, 1985; Teale and Sulzby, 1986; Bus, 1995). Similarly we may think of "emergent literary competence" by offering children an environment rich in stories that encourage meaningful structuring activities and by having "literary conversations" with them. At a later stage instruction can become more formal and children can learn to reflect on what they have learned tacitly so far.

At the ages of 4–6 most children are particularly interested to find out how things work. We only have to think of the many "why" or "how" questions they ask. Discovering the system(s) behind the events, a structuralist pursuit *par excellence*, therefore, will not only help make them competent readers of literature, but may also prove to be a source of endless literary discoveries.

Acknowledgment The 'Picture books and concept development' project (2005–2009) was funded by the Programme Council for Educational Research, part of the Netherlands Organisation for Scientific Research (NWO).

Open Access This article is distributed under the terms of the Creative Commons Attribution License which permits any use, distribution, and reproduction in any medium, provided the original author(s) and the source are credited.

References

Applebee, Arthur N. (1978). *The Child's Concept of Story. Ages Two to Seventeen.* Chicago: The University of Chicago Press.
Brooks, Peter. (1976). Competent Readers. Review of: *Structuralist Poetics. Structuralism, Linguistics, and the Study of Literature* by Jonathan Culler. *Diacritics, 6*(1), 23–26.
Burton, Virginia L. (1978/1942). *The Little House.* New York: Houghton Mifflin.
Bus, Adriana G. (1995). *Geletterde peuters en kleuters: Theorie en praktijk van ontluikende geletterdheid.* Amsterdam: Boom.
Bus, Adriana G., Van Ijzendoorn, Marinus H. and Pellegrini, Anthony D. (1995). Joint Book Reading Makes for Success in Learning to Read: A Meta-Analysis on Intergenerational Transmission of Literacy. *Review of Educational Research, 65*, 1–21.
Child, Lauren. (2005). *We Honestly can Look After Your Dog.* London: Penguin Books.
Chomsky, Noam. (1965). *Aspects of the Theory of Syntax.* Cambridge, MA: The MIT Press.
Cobb, Paul, Confrey, Jere, DiSessa, Andrea, Lehrer, Richard and Schauble, Leona. (2003). Design Experiments in Educational Research. *Educational Researcher, 32*(1), 9–13.
Culler, Jonathan. (2002/1975). *Structuralist Poetics: Structuralism, Linguistics and the Study of Literature.* London: Routledge.
Fish, Stanley. (1980). *Is There a Text in This Class? The Power of Interpretive Communities.* Cambridge MA: Harvard University Press.
Gravemeijer, Koeno and Cobb, Paul. (2006). Design Research from the Learning Design Perspective. In J. van den Akker, K. Gravemeijer, S. McKenney and N. Nieveen (Eds.), *Educational Design Research* (pp. 151–158). London: Routledge.
Gravett, Emily. (2005). *Wolves* London: Macmillan.
Kempter, Christa, and Weldin, Frauke. (2006). *Dear Little Lamb,.* New York: North South Books. (First published in Switzerland under the title *Liebes kleines Schaf,.* Dutch translation entitled: *Lief lammetje,.* Rijswijk: De Vier Windstreken.)
Kümmerling-Meibauer, Bettina. (1999). Metalinguistic Awareness and the Child's Developing Concept of Irony: The Relationship Between Pictures and Text in Ironic Picture Books. *The Lion and the Unicorn, 23*(2), 157–183.
Langer, Judith A. (1991). *Envisioning Literature: Literary Understanding and Literature Instruction.* Newark/New York: The International Reading Association/Teachers College Press.
Mackey, Margaret. (1993). Picture Books and the Making of Readers: A New Trajectory. *NCTE Concept Paper Series No. 7.* Urbana, IL: National Council of Teachers of English.
Meek, Margaret. (1996). *Information and Book Learning.* Stroud: Thimble Press.
Piaget, Jean. (1972). *The Child's Conception of the World.* Totowa, NJ: Littlefield Adams.
Sipe, Lawrence R. (2000). The Construction of Literary Understanding by First and Second Graders in Oral Response to Picture Storybook Read-Alouds. *Reading Research Quarterly, 35*(2), 252–275.
Stott, Jon C. (1982). "It's not What You Expect": Teaching Irony to Third Graders (Editorial View). *Children's Literature in Education, 13*(4), 153–163.
Sulzby, Elisabeth. (1985). Children's Emergent Reading of Favorite Storybooks: A Developmental Study. *Reading Research Quarterly, 20*(4), 458–481.
Teale, William and Sulzby, Elisabeth (Eds.). (1986). *Emergent Literacy: Writing and Reading.* Norwood, NJ: Ablex.
Van der Pol, Coosje. (2010). *Prentenboeken lezen als literatuur. Een structuralistische benadering van het concept 'literaire competentie' voor kleuters.* Amsterdam/Delft: Stichting Lezen/Eburon. (Doctoral thesis, in Dutch with a summary in English).
Verhoeven, Ludo, Aarnoutse, Cor, Blauw, Akke de, Boland, Theo, Vernooy, Kees, and Zandt, Regine van het. (1999). *Tussendoelen beginnende geletterdheid. Een leerlijn voor groep 1 tot en met 3.* Nijmegen: Expertisecentrum Nederlands.
Vis, Leendert Jan. (2000). *Jaap schaap.* Rotterdam: Lemniscaat.
Willis, Jeanne and Ross, Tony. (2007). *Cottonwool Colin.* London: Andersen Press. [Translated in Dutch: *Watje Wimpie.* Antwerpen: De Vries-Brouwers].

COMMEMORATIVE ISSUE FOR DR. LAWRENCE SIPE

Author Studies: An Effective Strategy for Engaging Pre-Service Teachers in the Study of Children's Literature

Amy Kennedy

Published online: 15 February 2012
© Springer Science+Business Media, LLC 2012

> I am really excited to share my author study with you today because I think he is a really cool guy and I think you are going to fall in love with him and his books as much as I did.

This quote could have been heard in just about any elementary classroom. Or perhaps from a middle-schooler who had just discovered a new favorite author thanks to his latest author study assignment. But it wasn't… it was spoken by a university student in her final year of classes.

What is an Author Study?

Author studies have been used for many years by teachers to introduce students to authors. They can be a powerful tool in motivating students to read and enticing students to try reading a genre or author that they might normally not choose. When I was a first grade teacher, I could tell which author the students were studying in library class by which books they would choose to take out or by which shelves were empty in the library. Author studies can encourage critical thinking by asking

---

Submission in honor of Dr. Lawrence Sipe.

Amy Kennedy is an assistant professor in elementary education at her undergraduate alma mater, Kutztown University. Prior to entering higher education, she was an elementary school classroom teacher for 13 years in Wilson School District in West Lawn, PA. A graduate of the University of Pennsylvania's M.S. Ed. Reading/Writing/Literacy program, she took every class with Dr. Sipe that she could fit into her schedule. She is currently a doctoral student at Widener University.

A. Kennedy (✉)
Kutztown University of Pennsylvania, Beekey Building 112, Kutztown, PA 19530, USA
e-mail: akennedy@kutztown.edu

A. Kennedy
571 Gaul Road, Sinking Spring, PA 19608, USA

students to make connections between an author's life and his books, to analyze texts and illustrations, and look for themes among several different books (Jenkins, 1999).

Author studies can be a whole class activity, group project, or individual assignment. In a whole group author study, a teacher may take the lead in presenting the author to the class. In my first grade classroom, we did many author studies this way. We would read, compare and contrast several books by the same author or illustrator and discuss the author's style and reoccurring themes. Then we would investigate biographical information and the author's website which usually provides a plethora of information. Lastly, using one of the author's books as an example of effective writing, we would produce our own story, either through shared writing or writer's workshop. We would try to stay as true to the author or author illustrator's style and form as possible while adding our own sense of creativity.

Students can also investigate authors in a group or as individuals. Author studies can be presented in many forms from posters to written biographies to PowerPoint or any other way students can imagine. Whether an author study is done as a whole class activity, in a small group, or individually, one of the greatest consequences of doing the author studies is that students begin to feel very attached to their author, as demonstrated by the quote at the beginning of this text. This can lead to students wanting to read additional works by their author, which is always a positive, unless of course you are doing a whole group author study and don't have enough books for every child. Another consequence could be heated classroom discussions in which students passionately defend their author as the best. Can you imagine the discussions? In a fifth grade classroom pitting Jerry Spinnelli against Katherine Paterson? Or first graders rooting for Mo Willems versus Eric Carle?

But What About in a College Classroom?

I first was introduced to the idea of author studies in the college classroom as a graduate student at the University of Pennsylvania. I was lucky enough to have Dr. Lawrence Sipe as my professor in children's literature. As a child I had been an avid reader, and I had great undergraduate experience in children's literature so I was already a fan, but it was Dr. Sipe that helped me realize that I wanted to be a professor of children's literature "when I grew up".

One of the most effective assignments from him was his author study assignment. He had each member of the class research an author from the list provided and create a one-page (front and back) handout containing, biographical information, a booklist, and notes on style/format, genre, and a critical commentary. Then we were to present the information to the class and provide each member of the class with a copy of the handout so that we would all be able to put together a binder of authors. Brilliant! I knew sitting there listening to my classmates' excitement over their authors that one day I would do this exact assignment with my own students. And I have.

The Assignment

Right now I teach undergraduate teacher candidates, usually in their final year, in what Kutztown University's department of Elementary Education terms "the professional semester" in which students take 8-weeks of classes on-campus, and then 8 weeks placed in an elementary school classroom to observe the expert teacher, help with small groups, participate in planning and implementing assigned lesson plans, and gain important classroom experience prior to student teaching. The children's literature course is one of six courses taught at that time period. The 8-weeks of on-campus course are quite intense, but a worthwhile trade-off when the students get to put recently acquired skills and knowledge to use right away. A big plus to having children's literature as part of the professional semester block of classes is that students have the books fresh in their minds and are able to share with teachers their newfound excitement for children's literature and bring them new books from our campus library that the teachers may not have access to through their school library.

I introduce the author study project during the very first class meeting time. They receive a cover sheet which explains the assignment, the rubric I will use to calculate their grade, and list of authors to choose from. Many of the students are unfamiliar with children's book authors, so I categorize the authors for the students by "novel" authors, "picture book" authors and illustrators, "multi-genre and form" for those authors who write an array of novels, picture books and poetry, informational book writers, and poets. Taking a cue from Dr. Sipe, I ask the students to choose an author that they are not already familiar with. I tell the students that if they aren't sure who to pick, that I can match them up with someone. This has worked very well. I will ask students to tell me what grade they like to teach, what genre they enjoy reading, and generally what they are interested in and I try to match them up with an author they will enjoy researching and reading. Some students will have no preference whatsoever and I like to choose an author for them to do their author study on; I use this opportunity to evenly distribute within genres and formats or include authors that I think are too important to miss.

I ask them to include a biography of their author and ask the students to include details about events that were important in terms of their inspiration for or development in becoming an author. For a class it is interesting to note similarities in authors' background stories. Students who choose an author or illustrator of picture books, including informational picture books by such authors as Aliki or Gail Gibbons, are asked to read 7–10 of that author/illustrator's books; those who read novels read a minimum of three. For authors who write both picture books and novels, as well as for poets, we negotiate how much they should read, depending on which books they find available. Students are asked to include an annotated bibliography for what they've read and include a list of other books by the author or illustrator, as complete as space will allow.

Students also need to include sections telling about their author's style, format, genre, and recurring themes. For some students this is the first time that they have been asked to look at a body of work critically. This makes the critical commentary section the most difficult to write for many of them. I try to move them beyond the idea of just saying that they just like or don't like to book. Using music as an example, I explain to the students that although they may not like opera or choose to listen to it on their own time, they could appreciate the talent it takes to be an opera singer and can certainly tell the difference between a high quality and a poor opera singer. I use the example of Susan Boyle from *Britain's Got Talent* to further explain my point. Even people who are not normally "fans" of her kind of singing could appreciate her amazing talent. And then we discuss how the deeper we delve in this course the more they will become experts in quality children's literature; as a musical judge can hear problems with pitch and tone that the normal person cannot, they will be able to become familiar with children's literature and will be able to recognize quality children's literature.

I show students examples of past author studies only from afar. I don't let them read them; I only show them so they can get a sense of the ways they can organize their author study on a page. My students have the advantage of being very techno savvy and can design high quality professional looking documents. Some students choose to design a tri-fold pamphlet, others have done newspaper style, and some make it like a print advertisement; I have been continuously impressed as the semesters pass with the quality and professionalism of the documents the students create.

Lastly, students need to make copies of the handout; one for myself and one for every member of the class and present their author to the class in 5 min (or less). This is the most effective part of this project's design. Students are thrilled to have their own "collection" of authors to reference. So in a class of 29 students, student will get to know 29 authors. The difficulty, however, is the time. Students can get so "into" their author that they have a hard part cutting themselves off. Nonetheless, seeing their joy at discovering an author, and how that joy can be truly infectious, it is truly time well spent.

Positive Experiences with Reading

College students can get as excited as elementary school children about children's books and children's book authors. We can get college students excited about reading again. And since research has demonstrated a link between teacher's personal reading habits and experiences and the quality of their literacy instruction in the classroom, inspiring pre-service teachers to love to read should be a goal for all teacher education programs.

More than 50% of my semester reviews from students mention the author study assignment as a positive aspect of my course; none mentions it as a negative. Even more telling, it is the only assignment that consistently, every semester has had at least one student ask me to do TWO author studies. Some of these students have chosen an author they are unfamiliar with and then their favorite author wasn't chosen so they feel compelled to do both as an author study; others have done preliminary research on two authors and can't choose between them, so they just do both. This project has been very successful in introducing pre-service teachers to a wide variety of authors to which they can introduce to their own students. It is an excellent model which my pre-service teachers can incorporate into their own classroom one day.

Reference

Jenkins, C.B. (1999). *The Allure of Authors*. Portsmouth, NH: Heinemann.

The manufacturer's authorised representative in the EU is Springer Nature Customer Service Centre GmbH, Europaplatz 3, 69115 Heidelberg, Germany. If you have any concerns regarding our products, please contact ProductSafety@springernature.com

Printed and bound by CPI Group (UK) Ltd, Croydon, CR0 4YY

25/03/2026

02078364-0006